PERFECT UNION

Where Identity, Intimacy, and Power Begin

I0517855

RANDY T. CURTIS, JR.

"But he who is joined to the Lord is one spirit with Him."
—1 Corinthians 6:17 (NKJV)

PERFECT UNION
Where Identity, Intimacy and Power Begin

Kingdom Publishing LLC
Odenton, MD 21113

Printed in the United States of America

ISBN: 978-1-967006-08-3

Table of Contents

DEDICATION

This book is dedicated to Yeshua, my Perfect Union—the One in whom I live, move, and have my being.

ACKNOWLEDGEMENTS

To the saints—the set-apart ones—who crave not merely information about God but living communion with Him: this work was birthed for you.

To my parents and faithful brothers in the Spirit who walked alongside me as the Lord taught me to abide—thank you for embodying a life of intimacy with Messiah. Your love, intercession, and example have been a steady anchor and a living witness of God's goodness.

To my beloved wife and children—your unwavering love, joy, and grace have been daily reflections of Messiah's faithfulness. Thank you for journeying with me, praying me through, and standing firm in the call. Your sacrifice is woven into every page.

And to every believer who has ever felt far, unworthy, or fractured—may the Spirit awaken you to the eternal reality that you are already united with the Lord, one spirit with Him.

INTRODUCTION:
THE DIVINE INVITATION

LIVING FROM UNION, NOT FOR IT

In an age consumed by performance, personal optimization, and relentless self-definition, the concept of union with Christ stands as a quiet revolution. It is not a call to become a better version of yourself, nor a spiritual technique to gain favor with God. It is a divine reality—one that announces, not a self-made ascent to God, but God's intentional descent into humanity for the purpose of union, restoration, and transformation. This union is not merely theological; it is ontological. It is not earned by merit, activated by emotional fervor, or accessed through intellectual assent—it is given by grace and received by faith.

The Apostle Paul expressed this profound reality when he wrote to the Ephesians that God "made us alive together with Christ... and raised us up together, and made us sit together in the heavenly places in Christ Jesus."[1] This is not poetic hyperbole but spiritual reality. The believer's union with Christ transcends time and space—it is an eternal reality with present implications. As theologian James S. Stewart observed, "Union with Christ, rather than justification or election or eschatology, or indeed any of the other great apostolic themes, is the real clue to an understanding of Paul's thought."[2] This profound reality revolutionizes our understanding of how God has chosen to manifest Himself in human experience.

Throughout Jesus' earthly ministry, His primary opposition did not come from pagans or political rulers, but from the religious elite—the Pharisees, scribes, and temple authorities. These were the gatekeepers of a system built on performance, hierarchy, and public appearance. They rejected Jesus not because He was irreligious, but because He revealed a union with the Father that bypassed their structures and exposed their hypocrisy. "You have made the commandment of God of no effect by your tradition," He told them (Matthew 15:6). Jesus shook the foundation of religious performance by offering intimacy with God through Himself.

Biblical scholar N.T. Wright notes, "Jesus' critique of the Temple was not that it was 'too Jewish' but that it was not Jewish enough: it had failed to be the light to the nations which Isaiah had spoken of."[4] The Temple was intended to be the meeting place between God and humanity, but had become a barrier rather than a bridge. Jesus came to be the true Temple—the place where divine presence dwells fully and is accessible to all who come in faith.

Jesus launched a movement not from the temple steps, but in homes, hillsides, and wilderness places. It was an underground revolution—empowered by the Spirit, marked by authority, and aimed at the heart. He trained ordinary men and women to carry divine presence, healing, and proclamation without the approval of institutional religion. After His resurrection, this Spirit-empowered movement continued through the apostles, who carried the message of union to synagogues, cities, and Gentile households. They, too, faced the same religious resistance that crucified Jesus, yet they did not build new hierarchies— they built living communities grounded in love, truth, and the presence of Christ.

The Book of Acts records this phenomenon with remarkable clarity: "And with great power the apostles gave witness to the resurrection of the Lord Jesus. And great grace was upon them all."[5] This grace was not merely divine favor but divine presence—the reality of Christ living in and through His people. As scholar F.F. Bruce observes, "The community of believers was not simply a society of like-minded individuals; it was the body of Christ, indwelt by His Spirit."[6]

This battle remains today. Much of the modern church has again become entangled in image over intimacy, structure over Spirit, performance over presence. But Christ still calls. Not to a new system, but to the same union He offered from the beginning: "Abide in Me, and I in you" (John 15:4).

This book seeks to explore the meaning and magnitude of that union, especially as articulated in Scripture and preserved through the testimonies of early believers, apostles, and thoughtful theological voices. Union with Christ is not a secondary blessing. It is not a metaphor for closeness. It is the heart of redemption itself—the very reason for the Incarnation, crucifixion, resurrection, and glorification of the Messiah.

As theologian T.F. Torrance writes, "Union with Christ is the central truth of the whole doctrine of salvation... All other aspects of salvation can be rightly understood only in relation to union with Christ."[7] This book aims to recover this central emphasis and explore its implications for every dimension of the Christian life.

RECOVERING A LOST EMPHASIS

In much of Western Christianity, union with Christ has been eclipsed by forensic categories of salvation: guilt and innocence, punishment and pardon. While the legal aspects of salvation are indeed part of the biblical witness, they do not constitute its fullness. A legal pardon may remove guilt, but it does not confer life. Union with Christ does. As Michael Gorman notes, "Justification is not the center of Paul's theology. Participation in Christ is."[8]

This insight is not new. Many Christian thinkers throughout history have recognized this emphasis. John Clayton, for instance, wrote, "We must understand that as long as Christ remains outside of us, and we are separated from him, all that he has suffered and done for the salvation of the human race remains useless and of no value for us."[9] For Clayton, justification was not merely a legal declaration but the result of being united with Christ.

Irenaeus of Lyons wrote, "The Word of God, our Lord Jesus Christ, who did, through His transcendent love, become what we are, that He might bring us to be even what He is Himself."[10] This exchange motif—God becoming human so humans might participate in divine life—became central to patristic soteriology.

Union is participation in the divine life. It is not self-actualization, but Christ-realization. It is not a technique, but a transformation. It is not a program of moral reform, but a relational reconfiguration of the believer's very being. The believer does not merely belong to Christ; the believer exists in Christ (2 Corinthians 5:17). This distinction is seismic.

Biblical scholar Constantine Campbell, after extensive study of the Pauline "in Christ" language, concludes: "Union with Christ is the profound and mysterious reality by which God saves and transforms the believer in Christ... It affects the believer's relationship to God, status before God, identity and self-understanding, relationship to sin, relationship to other believers, and eschatological participation in the life of the coming age."[11] In other words, every aspect of salvation is grounded in this fundamental reality.

THE BIBLICAL PATTERN OF ONENESS

From the earliest chapters of Genesis, we find God's desire for relational union. Adam and Eve walked with God in the garden, not as servants merely executing commands, but as partners bearing His image and stewarding His creation (Genesis 1:26-28; 3:8). The fall fractured this union, introducing death, division, and distance. But even in the midst of judgment, God initiated the plan of restoration—not through detached forgiveness, but through redemptive indwelling.

The Book of 1 Enoch, widely read in the Second Temple period, expands on this theme: "And the Lord said to Michael: Go, bind Semjaza and his associates... In those days they shall be led off to the abyss of fire... And destroy all the spirits of the reprobate and the children of the Watchers, because they have wronged mankind. Destroy all wrong from the face of the earth... And all the righteous shall become the elect ones" (1 Enoch 10:11-17). This text shows how early believers understood the fall as cosmic disruption requiring divine restoration.

Throughout the Hebrew Scriptures, the presence of God among His people is seen as the ultimate blessing. The tabernacle and temple are not merely sites of ritual—they are dwelling places of divine presence (Exodus 25:8; 29:45-46; 1 Kings 8:10-11). Yet even these structures foreshadowed something more intimate. The prophetic vision was not merely God with His people, but God within His people (Ezekiel 36:26-27; Jeremiah 31:33).

The Dead Sea Scrolls reflect this hope for internalized divine presence. In the Community Rule (1QS), we find expectations of God placing "a spirit of holiness" within the faithful remnant: "Then God will purify by His truth all the deeds of man... to cleanse him through a holy spirit from all wicked practices, sprinkling upon him a spirit of truth" (1QS 4:20-21). This anticipates the New Covenant promise of internal transformation rather than mere external observance.

This promise finds its fulfillment in Christ, not only as the Messiah, but as the vessel through whom God brings about the indwelling of His Spirit. The New Covenant does not merely upgrade the externalities of religious life—it internalizes the very presence and law of God within the believer. As Paul declares, "Do you not know that Jesus Christ is in you?" (2 Corinthians 13:5).

The Gospel of John particularly emphasizes this theme of mutual indwelling. Jesus prays for his followers, "that they all may be one, as You, Father, are in Me, and I in You; that they also may be one in Us" (John 17:21). This is not merely unity of purpose but a genuine spiritual union—believers united with Christ as Christ is united with the Father.

UNION AS PARTICIPATION, NOT PANTHEISM

Union with Christ is not the erasure of personhood. It is not absorption into a cosmic whole or loss of individuality. Rather, it is the elevation of the believer's humanity through divine participation. Just as Jesus maintained His unique personhood while being perfectly united with the Father in will, so too the believer maintains personhood while being united with Christ in spirit (John 17:21-23).

Introduction

Peter speaks of believers becoming "partakers of the divine nature" (2 Peter 1:4)—a staggering statement that demands contemplation. This is not pantheism, nor is it the blurring of Creator and creation. It is the mystery of divine hospitality. God invites us into communion, not competition; into transformation, not transcendence.

Biblical scholar Richard Bauckham writes of 2 Peter 1:4, "This is not, as in pagan religion, the divinization of human beings, but their transformation by participation in the life of God."[14] The distinction is crucial. Union with Christ does not make believers divine; it enables them to participate in divine life through relationship.

This mystical union does not require speculative theology to access. It is the lived reality of the Spirit-filled believer. As the apostle John writes, "By this we know that we abide in Him and He in us, because He has given us of His Spirit" (1 John 4:13).

Theologian Karl Barth described this reality as "the heart of the whole Christian proclamation and of all Christian faith."[15] It is not an esoteric teaching for spiritual elites but the fundamental reality of Christian existence.

UNION IN EARLY BELIEVING COMMUNITIES

The earliest disciples understood union not as a concept to be defended but as a reality to be experienced. The writings of Paul, John, and others in the New Testament bear frequent witness to the language of being "in Christ," walking as one with Him, and bearing His image (Romans 6:3-5; Galatians 3:27-28; 1 John 2:5-6).

New Testament scholar Markus Bockmuehl observes, "For Paul, to be 'in Christ' is not a metaphor but a reality of existence... It implies a real participation in Christ's death and resurrection."[16] This understanding permeated early Christian communities and shaped their self-understanding as the body of Christ.

The Eastern concept of *theosis* reflects a stream of early interpretation. As Vladimir Lossky describes, "The union of the believer with God is not symbolic or ethical, but real—by grace and in truth."[17] While Western traditions tended to focus on legal righteousness, the East emphasized ontological participation—a union that renews the whole being.

Athanasius famously stated, "The Word became human so that humans might participate in the divine nature."[18] This statement, while striking to modern ears, was not proposing human deification but expressing the profound truth that through Christ, believers participate in divine life. It is transformation through relationship.

Even the Didache, one of the earliest Christian documents outside the New Testament, speaks of believers sharing in "spiritual food and drink and eternal life through Your servant."[19] This sacramental understanding points to a real participation in Christ's life, not merely symbolic remembrance.

This book draws on such insights not to endorse every associated theology, but to honor the shared scriptural vision for communion with God through the Messiah.

AN INVITATION TO LIVE AWAKE

Union is not something to strive toward—it is something to awaken to. We begin this book not with a call to *do*, but a call to see. Christ is not far off, nor is union with Him a future attainment. It is the present inheritance of every Spirit-filled believer. As Jesus said, "Abide in Me, and I in you" (John 15:4).

This abiding is not passive. It is the most vital and intentional form of spiritual awareness. It reshapes prayer from petition to presence. It reorients worship from performance to participation. It turns suffering from a curse into communion. And it transforms holiness from being only law-keeping into life-sharing.

Brother Lawrence, the 17th-century monk known for his "practice of the presence of God," embodied this awareness. He wrote, "The time of business does not with me differ from the time of prayer; and in the noise and clatter of my kitchen, while several persons are at the same time calling for different things, I possess God in as great tranquility as if I were upon my knees at the blessed sacrament."[20] This is union lived out in the mundane moments of everyday life.

Contemporary spiritual writer James Finley describes this awakening: "Union with Christ is not something we achieve but something we discover has already been achieved and is waiting for us to wake up to it."[21] This awakening transforms not only one's spiritual practices but one's entire way of being in the world.

May the chapters that follow awaken you to this truth—not as an abstract doctrine, but as a lived encounter with the Living Christ. For in Him we live, and move, and have our being (Acts 17:28).

CHAPTER 1

JESUS AND THE FATHER—A PERFECT MODEL OF UNION

The relationship between Jesus and the Father reveals the ultimate pattern of human beings joined to divine union. This is not a mystery of separate persons but a revelation of how God chose to manifest Himself in human form. Jesus's relationship with the Father, as recorded throughout the Gospels, demonstrates perfect unity of will, purpose, and divine presence manifested in human experience.

I. A SCRIPTURAL PORTRAIT OF UNION: "I AND THE FATHER ARE ONE"

Jesus plainly declared, "I and the Father are one" (John 10:30). This statement caused an uproar among the religious authorities—not merely because of its audacity, but because it pointed to a unity that transcended earthly categories. The Greek word used here, *hen*, denotes unity of essence and purpose.[22] Yet Jesus clarifies the nature of this oneness in numerous places. In John 14:28, He states, "The Father is greater than I," not as a contradiction, but as an affirmation of the relationship between God's transcendent nature and His manifestation in human form.

Biblical scholar Andreas Köstenberger notes that this unity is "both essential and functional—Jesus shares divine nature while perfectly submitting to divine will."[23] This understanding helps us see how God could manifest fully in human form while maintaining the reality of that human experience.

In John 5:19, Jesus declares, "The Son can do nothing of Himself, but what He sees the Father do." His words affirm that His actions flow from perfect alignment with divine will. Jesus doesn't claim to act independently but as the perfect human manifestation of God's presence and purpose.

This union demonstrates perfect relational harmony. Jesus reveals God not as a separate entity but as God's own self-expression in human form. His miracles, teachings, and authority flow from this perfect manifestation: "My teaching is not Mine, but His who sent Me" (John 7:16).

Isaiah foresaw this relationship when he spoke of the Servant who would be upheld and anointed by God (Isaiah 42:1). Jesus fulfills this pattern by perfectly manifesting God's presence in human form. He is the image of the invisible God (Colossians 1:15), and the exact imprint of His nature (Hebrews 1:3), because He reveals God without distortion.

II. THE DOCTRINE OF AGENCY IN THE SECOND TEMPLE WORLDVIEW

The Second Temple period was deeply shaped by concepts of divine representation and agency, as evidenced in texts from Qumran and other Second Temple literature. In the Dead Sea Scrolls, particularly in texts like 11QMelchizedek and 4Q491, we find developed ideas of divine agents who carry full authority from God while remaining unified with His purpose.

The Wisdom of Solomon describes Wisdom as God's agent: "She is a breath of the power of God, and a pure emanation of the glory of the Almighty... For she is a reflection of eternal light, a spotless mirror of the working of God, and an image of his goodness" (Wisdom 7:25-26). This framework of divine agency helps us understand how Jesus could fully manifest God's presence and authority.

In 1 Enoch, the "Son of Man" figure acts with divine authority: "And in that hour that Son of Man was named in the presence of the Lord of Spirits... All who dwell on earth shall fall down and worship before him" (1 Enoch 48:2-5). This shows how Second Temple texts conceived of God manifesting His authority through chosen vessels.

This framework is essential to understanding Jesus' declarations about His relationship with the Father. When He says, "Whoever receives Me receives Him who sent Me" (Matthew 10:40) or "He who has seen Me has seen the Father" (John 14:9), He speaks as God's perfect manifestation in human form. In the Second Temple mind, such statements indicated complete divine authority and presence.

This model is consistent with how YHWH operated through chosen vessels in Scripture:

- Moses was made "as God" to Pharaoh (Exodus 7:1), manifesting divine authority.

- The prophets were called to speak on God's behalf, with His words in their mouths (Jeremiah 1:9).

- The Angel of YHWH appeared throughout Scripture with divine authority, sometimes speaking directly as God (Genesis 16:7-13).

Jesus fulfills and surpasses these patterns. As the uniquely begotten Son (John 1:18), He embodies the fullness of divine presence with perfect unity of purpose. His relationship with the Father demonstrates perfect harmony in will, mission, and nature.

III. THE DYNAMIC OF OBEDIENCE AND DEPENDENCE

A key hallmark of Jesus's unity with the Father is His unwavering obedience. "I do nothing on My own authority, but speak just as the Father taught Me" (John 8:28). This obedience is not mechanical but relational. It arises from perfect alignment with divine will. "The Father loves the Son and shows Him all things that He Himself is doing" (John 5:20). Here we see divine unity expressed through perfect harmony of purpose.

Contemporary theologian Miroslav Volf observes, "Jesus' obedience to the Father is the perfect expression of divine unity manifested in human experience. It shows us how human life can be perfectly aligned with divine purpose."[26]

This dependence was especially evident during the most trying moment of Jesus's earthly life—the Garden of Gethsemane. "Not My will, but Yours be done" (Luke 22:42). In submitting to divine will unto death, Jesus demonstrated that true union is expressed in complete surrender. His humanity revealed the perfection of divine purpose.

This model has profound implications for the believer. As Jesus lived in perfect alignment with God's will, we are called to live in union with Him. The obedience He exemplified becomes the template for our own life in Christ—not as legalistic compliance, but as relational unity. "Whoever keeps His word, truly the love of God is perfected in him. By this we know that we are in Him" (1 John 2:5).

IV. JESUS AS THE IMAGE OF GOD

To understand Jesus is to understand God's intention for humanity. In Him, the fullness of God dwells bodily (Colossians 2:9), not merely as an abstract deity, but in the person of a man who lived, walked, suffered, and overcame. Jesus is "the image of the invisible God" (Colossians 1:15), the One who makes God known (John 1:18).

When Philip asked, "Lord, show us the Father," Jesus replied, "Have I been with you so long, and you still do not know Me? ... He who has seen Me has seen the Father" (John 14:8-9). This was a revelation of perfect manifestation. Jesus is the window through which the character, intentions, and love of God are displayed.

The prophets longed to see what the disciples saw. In Christ, the mystery hidden for ages was made manifest (Colossians 1:26). His unity with the divine revealed that God's ultimate goal was not simply to dwell among His people—but to dwell within them (Ezekiel 36:27; 2 Corinthians 6:16).

V. THE HIGH PRIESTLY PRAYER: THE VISION FOR SHARED UNION

In John 17, Jesus prays what is often called the High Priestly Prayer. This intercession, spoken on the eve of His crucifixion, reveals His deepest desires for those who would believe in Him: "That they all may be one, just as You, Father, are in Me, and I in You, that they also may be in Us" (John 17:21).

Here, Jesus expresses not only His oneness with God but His desire to extend that union to His followers. This is not a metaphor but a mission. Jesus does not pray that we would merely agree doctrinally, but that we would share in the same divine communion that He enjoys. "I in them and You in Me, that they may become perfectly one" (John 17:23).

This vision of shared union is echoed by Paul, who writes, "He who is joined to the Lord is one spirit with Him" (1 Corinthians 6:17). This joining is not progressive but positional—it is the reality of every believer who has received the Spirit of God.

VI. IMPLICATIONS FOR THE BELIEVER

To understand the unity between Jesus and the Father is to lay the foundation for understanding the believer's union with Christ. As Jesus was never separated from divine purpose, so the believer is never apart from Christ. "I am with you always, even to the end of the age" (Matthew 28:20). The indwelling Spirit is the witness and guarantee of this communion (Romans 8:9-11).

This union transforms the believer's approach to spiritual life. No longer do we strive to earn God's presence; we abide in what is already true. No longer do we perform to be accepted; we live from acceptance. No longer do we labor to prove ourselves worthy; we rest in the worthiness of the One in whom we dwell.

Union with Christ is the answer to the fragmented identity, moral striving, and spiritual isolation that plague so many believers today. It is the revelation that we are not alone, not deficient, not distant. We are one spirit with the Lord.

CHAPTER 2

THE BIBLICAL BASIS FOR OUR UNION
WITH CHRIST

FROM IMAGE-BEARING TO INDWELLING

Union with Christ is not a theological abstraction—it is a revealed and repeatable pattern woven throughout the entire narrative of Scripture. From the creation account to the final vision of the New Jerusalem, the consistent thread is God's desire not merely to be known about, but to be known intimately—dwelling with and within His people. This union is not poetic language. It is the central promise of the gospel: that humanity, once alienated from God, can now be restored, not merely to moral innocence, but to divine communion.

As John Murray, one of the 20th century's foremost Reformed theologians, stated: "Nothing is more central or basic than union with Christ... Union with Christ is really the central truth of the whole doctrine of salvation not only in its application but also in its once-for-all accomplishment in the finished work of Christ."[30]

I. UNION FORESHADOWED IN CREATION AND COVENANT

The human story begins with intimacy. In Genesis 2:7, the LORD God "formed the man of dust from the ground and breathed into his nostrils the breath of life." The result was not merely animation—it was communion. The Hebrew word for "breathed" *(napach)* appears rarely in Scripture and suggests

17

intimate, personal action.[31] Humanity was made in the "image and likeness of God" (Genesis 1:26-27), a unique status not shared by any other creature. The image of God is not merely a rational or moral capacity—it is a relational call to reflect, receive, and reveal God's presence on earth.

Old Testament scholar Gerhard von Rad notes, "The image of God is not primarily about human attributes but about human relationship to God. Humans are God's representatives on earth, which implies both dignity and intimate connection."[32]

Adam and Eve walked with God in the garden (Genesis 3:8), signifying a level of relational proximity that was broken through disobedience. Yet even after the fall, the redemptive trajectory of Scripture is toward reunion. From the calling of Abraham (Genesis 12:1-3) to the construction of the tabernacle (Exodus 25:8) and the prophetic promise of a new heart and Spirit (Ezekiel 36:26-27), God's consistent aim is to dwell among His people.

The Book of Jubilees, a Second Temple text, emphasizes this theme of divine presence: "And I shall dwell with them throughout all the ages of eternity. And I shall reveal to them My face and they shall see Me" (Jubilees 1:26). This reflects the deep longing within Second Temple Judaism for restored intimacy with God.

The covenantal language of "I will be their God, and they shall be My people" (Jeremiah 31:33) reveals not just ownership, but union. God covenants to live with His faithful remnant, those who keep His commandments. The union motif continues through the Hebrew prophets, who speak of God "marrying" His people (Hosea 2:19-20; Isaiah 54:5), pointing to a relational oneness fulfilled in the Messiah.

II. JESUS AS THE FULFILLMENT OF UNION PROPHECIES

Jesus is not an interruption to the biblical narrative—He is its fulfillment. As Emmanuel, "God with us" (Matthew 1:23), He inaugurates a new kind of presence: one that does not dwell in tents or temples made by human hands, but in flesh and blood. John affirms, "The Word became flesh and dwelt among us" (John 1:14). The Greek term *eskēnōsen* ("dwelt") literally means "tabernacled," linking Jesus to the dwelling presence of God in the wilderness.[33]

Scholar Craig Keener observes, "John deliberately uses tabernacle language to show that Jesus embodies what the temple represented—the dwelling place of God's glory among His people."[34]

More than this, Jesus came to give life—a new kind of life not external to the believer, but internal. "I have come that they may have life, and that they may have it more abundantly" (John 10:10). This abundant life is not material comfort but spiritual communion. Jesus prayed, "Just as You, Father, are in Me and I in You, that they also may be in Us" (John 17:21). His life was not only an atonement for sin but a conduit for restored union.

The Gospel of John is especially rich with the language of union. Jesus says, "I am the vine, you are the branches. He who abides in Me, and I in him, bears much fruit" (John 15:5). This is not metaphorical in a literary sense—it is descriptive of spiritual reality. To be "in Christ" is not to be associated with Him externally but to be joined to Him internally.

19

III. PAULINE THEOLOGY: "IN CHRIST" AS CORE IDENTITY

Paul's letters form the most detailed exposition of the believer's union with Christ. The phrase "in Christ," "in Him," or "in the Lord" occurs over 160 times in the Pauline corpus.[35] This is not rhetorical flourish—it is Paul's entire understanding of salvation. To be justified is to be "in Christ" (Galatians 2:17). To be sanctified is to be "in Christ Jesus, who became for us wisdom from God—and righteousness and sanctification and redemption" (1 Corinthians 1:30). To be a new creation is to be "in Christ" (2 Corinthians 5:17).

James D.G. Dunn, a leading Pauline scholar, writes: "For Paul, being 'in Christ' is not a metaphor but the most real fact about Christian existence. It describes a sphere of influence, a corporate personality, and a mystical union all at once."[36]

Union is not a post-conversion add-on; it is the essence of conversion. Romans 6:3-5 declares that all who were baptized into Christ were baptized into His death and resurrection. "We have been united together in the likeness of His death, certainly we also shall be in the likeness of His resurrection." This language is not symbolic. It is ontological. The believer has died with Christ, been buried with Him, and now lives in Him.

In Galatians 2:20, Paul writes, "I have been crucified with Christ; it is no longer I who live, but Christ lives in me." This is not mystical pantheism but radical identification. The believer's former self has been replaced by Christ's indwelling presence. Ephesians 2:6 expands this further: "And raised us up together, and made us sit together in the heavenly places in Christ Jesus." Even now, our spiritual position is one of union with the ascended Messiah.

IV. METAPHORS OF UNION IN THE NEW TESTAMENT

The New Testament employs several rich metaphors to describe union with Christ. Each image reveals a distinct facet of this glorious mystery:

- **The Vine and the Branches** (John 15:1-8): Emphasizes organic dependence. The branch has no life apart from the vine. Union is not optional—it is vital. Scholar D.A. Carson notes, "The organic metaphor stresses that spiritual fruitfulness is impossible apart from vital connection to Christ."[37]

- **The Body and Its Members** (1 Corinthians 12:12-27): Highlights shared function and interdependence. Each believer is joined not only to Christ but to one another. Paul's use of the body metaphor emphasizes, as Gordon Fee observes, "the corporate nature of our union with Christ—we cannot be 'in Christ' without being connected to His body."[38]

- **The Temple and Its Living Stones** (Ephesians 2:19-22; 1 Peter 2:5): Focuses on collective indwelling. God now dwells not in buildings but in people. Peter T. O'Brien comments, "The temple metaphor shows that believers collectively form the dwelling place of God through the Spirit."[39]

- **The Bride and the Bridegroom** (Ephesians 5:31-32; Revelation 21:2): Underscores intimate love, covenant loyalty, and anticipated union in fullness. This metaphor, as Anthony Thiselton notes, "captures the personal, intimate, and permanent nature of our relationship with Christ."[40]

Each metaphor reveals union as both individual and corporate, invisible yet transformative, grounded in Christ and sustained by the Spirit.

V. THE ROLE OF THE SPIRIT IN UNION

While Christ is the object of our union, the Spirit is the means by which we experience God's presence. Paul declares, "Anyone who does not have the Spirit of Christ does not belong to Him" (Romans 8:9). The Spirit is not merely a helper from without, but the indwelling presence of God within. "Do you not know that your bodies are temples of the Holy Spirit who is in you, whom you have received from God?" (1 Corinthians 6:19).

Theologian Sinclair Ferguson explains, "The Spirit's work is to unite us to Christ and to make real in our experience what Christ has accomplished for us. The Spirit is the means of our experiential union with Christ."[41]

Through the Spirit, believers cry "Abba, Father!" (Romans 8:15), not as detached servants but as children united to God. The Spirit bears witness that we are children of God and "heirs— heirs of God and co-heirs with Christ" (Romans 8:17). This inheritance is not only future glory but present

VI. A NEW HUMANITY IN CHRIST

Union with Christ is the formation of a new human race. "For as in Adam all die, even so in Christ all shall be made alive" (1 Corinthians 15:22). Christ is not merely the Redeemer of individuals—He is the head of a new creation (Colossians

1:18). Those who are in Him constitute a new kind of humanity, reconciled to God and to one another.

N.T. Wright elaborates: "Paul's vision is not just individual salvation but the creation of a new humanity in Christ. The church is not a collection of saved individuals but a corporate entity that embodies the new creation."[42]

Paul writes, "You have put off the old man with his deeds, and have put on the new man who is renewed in knowledge according to the image of Him who created him" (Colossians 3:9-10). This echoes Genesis but surpasses it. The new creation does not merely reflect God—it contains God. "Christ in you, the hope of glory" (Colossians 1:27).

Union with Christ means the believer is no longer separated as inferior by ethnicity, status, or gender, but by spiritual identity: "There is neither Jew nor Greek... male nor female, for you are all one in Christ Jesus" (Galatians 3:28).

CHAPTER 3

UNION WITH CHRIST—IDENTITY BEFORE ACTIVITY

BECOMING BY BEING, NOT BY DOING

One of the most revolutionary truths of the gospel is that who we are in Christ is not determined by what we do, but what He has done. In a religious culture steeped in effort, performance, and spiritual striving, the doctrine of union with Christ re-centers the believer's life around divine identity rather than human activity. It declares that we do not labor *to become accepted,* holy, righteous, or complete—we act *because we already are.*

Union with Christ is not the reward of spiritual maturity; it is the root of our spiritual life. Every command of the New Testament assumes the believer's position in Christ before addressing their practice. Paul's epistles, for instance, almost always begin with declarations of identity—"saints," "called," "beloved," "in Christ"—before issuing any imperatives for behavior.

As Robert Letham observes, "Union with Christ is the foundation of all the blessings of salvation. The Christian life in its entirety is rooted in our union with Christ."[43] This reality fundamentally reorients our understanding of the Christian life from performance-based religion to relationship-based transformation.

I. IDENTITY ESTABLISHED AT CONVERSION

When a person is born again, something greater than a change in belief occurs: a transformation in being. This is why Paul says, "If anyone is in Christ, he is a new creation; old things have passed away; behold, all things have become new" (2 Corinthians 5:17). This is not future hope but present reality. The believer does not simply receive forgiveness—they receive a new identity.

The language of Scripture regarding this transformation is decisive and categorical. In Romans 6:6, Paul writes, "knowing this, that our old man was crucified with Him, that the body of sin might be done away with, that we should no longer be slaves of sin." The verb "was crucified" (συνεσταυρώθη, synestaurōthē) is in the aorist tense, indicating a completed action.[44] The believer's old identity has already been put to death with Christ.

Paul reinforces this in Colossians 3:3: "For you died, and your life is hidden with Christ in God." The old self—the identity defined by sin, shame, and striving—has been crucified with Christ (Galatians 2:20). A new identity now emerges, one no longer defined by earthly credentials but heavenly union.

Theologian John Murray articulates this reality powerfully: "Nothing is more central or basic than union and communion with Christ.... Union with Christ is really the central truth of the whole doctrine of salvation."[45] This union is not metaphorical but mystical and actual—a genuine spiritual reality that transforms the very core of human identity.

This reality is foundational. Every struggle with sin, fear, insecurity, and legalism can be traced back to a failure to grasp our identity in Christ. If the believer truly knows they are "accepted in the Beloved" (Ephesians 1:6), they no longer need to labor for human acceptance. If they understand they are "seated in heavenly places in Christ Jesus" (Ephesians 2:6), they cease striving for status or spiritual rank.

Biblical scholar F.F. Bruce notes, "Our identification with Christ in his death and resurrection... means our death to the old order and our rising to the new order."[46] This new order is not achieved through religious effort but received through spiritual rebirth.

II. ALREADY HOLY, ALREADY COMPLETE

The New Testament writers speak of believers in terms that reflect a completed identity, not a future ideal. Consider the radical declarations:

- "You are complete in Him" (Colossians 2:10)

- "You are the temple of God" (1 Corinthians 3:16)

- "You were washed... sanctified... justified" (1 Corinthians 6:11)

- "You are light in the Lord" (Ephesians 5:8)

- "You have the mind of Christ" (1 Corinthians 2:16)

These are not motivational metaphors—they are statements of spiritual reality. The believer is not on a ladder of spiritual progression, climbing higher each day. Instead, they begin from fullness and live from that fullness. As Peter writes, "His divine power has given to us all things that pertain to life and godliness" (2 Peter 1:3). Nothing is missing. The journey of sanctification

27

is not gaining more of God, but allowing more of Him to be revealed through us.

Augustine wrote, "The Christian should be an alleluia from head to foot."[47] This joyful reality stems not from achievement but from identity. We are not becoming holy—we are holy ones (saints) learning to live out our holiness.

Hebrews 10:14 declares, "For by one offering He has perfected forever those who are being sanctified." Here we find the paradox: the believer is both perfected and being sanctified. The perfection refers to the believer's identity in Christ—unchanging, whole, holy. The sanctification process is the outward working of that inward reality.

Theologian Sinclair Ferguson expresses this beautifully: "Sanctification is the art of getting used to your justification."[48] In other words, the Christian life is not about becoming what we're not yet, but becoming in practice what we already are in position.

The implications of this are profound. No longer must the believer strive anxiously for divine approval—they already possess it in Christ. As Paul affirms in Romans 8:1, "There is therefore now no condemnation to those who are in Christ Jesus." The absence of condemnation is not conditional upon performance but established through position.

III. FROM STRIVING TO ABIDING

Jesus's words in John 15 are pivotal: "Abide in Me, and I in you... without Me you can do nothing" (John 15:4-5). The word "abide" (Greek: *meno*) means to remain, dwell, or continue. It is a call not to effort, but to awareness; not to striving, but to staying.

Biblical scholar D.A. Carson explains, "The branches do not have to try to produce fruit. All they are asked to do is to remain in connection with the vine... The vital thing is not self-conscious effort but the constant connection of the believer to Christ."[49] This connection is maintained through faith, not religious exertion.

Fruitfulness in the kingdom does not come from exertion but connection. The branch does not strain to bear fruit—it simply remains in the vine. The same is true for the believer. Activity in the kingdom must be the overflow of abiding identity. Ministry, prayer, obedience, and holiness are not pathways to union but expressions of it.

The prophet Isaiah anticipated this reality: "You will keep him in perfect peace, whose mind is stayed on You, because he trusts in You" (Isaiah 26:3). The Hebrew word for "stayed" (סָמַךְ, samak) carries the sense of leaning upon or resting weight upon something.[50] The peaceful, fruitful Christian life comes not through self-effort but through resting weight upon God.

This shift—from striving to abiding—liberates the believer from performance anxiety. No longer is spiritual life about measuring up. It becomes about yielding to the One who lives within. "The life I now live in the flesh I live by faith in the Son of God" (Galatians 2:20). Faith does not energize human effort; it surrenders to divine presence.

Dallas Willard captures this reality: "Grace is not opposed to effort; it's opposed to earning."[51] The believer does not cease from activity—they cease from anxiety-driven achievement. Their doing flows from their being.

IV. SONSHIP BEFORE SERVICE

Jesus modeled this principle perfectly. Before He performed any miracle, cast out any demon, or preached any sermon, He heard the voice from heaven: "This is My beloved Son, in whom I am well pleased" (Matthew 3:17). Identity preceded ministry. Approval came before performance.

This order is essential. Jesus's ministry flowed from divine identity, not toward it. Likewise, we serve not to gain God's pleasure but from it. "As the Father has loved Me, so I have loved you. Abide in My love" (John 15:9). The power to walk in obedience comes not from fear of rejection, but from confidence in union.

Theologian J.I. Packer writes, "Our high status as children and heirs of God through Christ (Gal. 4:4-7) should be the basis of our whole life."[52] This status is not earned through service but received through grace.

Paul identifies believers as "sons" and "heirs" through Christ (Galatians 4:7). This status is not achieved through service—it is received through the Spirit. "Because you are sons, God has sent forth the Spirit of His Son into your hearts, crying out, 'Abba, Father!'" (Galatians 4:6). Our identity as children of God secures us in divine love and positions us for faithful activity.

In his classic work "The Prodigal God," Timothy Keller notes, "The gospel is this: We are more sinful and flawed in ourselves than we ever dared believe, yet at the very same time we are more loved and accepted in Christ than we ever dared hope."[53] This dual reality—our complete unworthiness apart from Christ and our complete worthiness in Him—forms the foundation of authentic Christian living.

The Scriptures frequently employ the language of adoption to describe this new relationship. In Romans 8:15, Paul writes, "For you did not receive the spirit of bondage again to fear, but you received the Spirit of adoption by whom we cry out, 'Abba, Father.'" The term "Abba" reflects intimate, familial relationship—not distant religious obligation.[54]

V. WALKING WORTHY OF WHO YOU ALREADY ARE

Paul urges believers to "walk worthy of the calling with which you were called" (Ephesians 4:1). Note the language: the walk follows the calling; the behavior follows the identity. Holiness, compassion, faithfulness, and fruitfulness are not prerequisites for union—they are responses to it.

New Testament scholar Klyne Snodgrass observes, "The imperative rests on the indicative. That is, the command is based on the reality of what God has done... Ethical living is a response to grace, not a prerequisite for it."[55] This pattern recurs throughout Paul's writings—statement of identity precedes instruction for activity.

This reframes spiritual disciplines. Bible study is no longer a means of trying to earn favor; it becomes a way of aligning with truth. Prayer is not a religious obligation but an act of union and intimacy. Fasting is not about proving devotion but creating space to feast on the life of Christ.

The writer of Hebrews captures this beautifully: "Let us draw near with a true heart in full assurance of faith, having our hearts sprinkled from an evil conscience and our bodies washed with pure water" (Hebrews 10:22). The invitation to "draw near" is based on cleansing already received, not cleansing yet to be earned.

When believers internalize their identity in Christ, obedience becomes natural, worship becomes joyful, and evangelism becomes relational. The spiritual life is not imposed—it is expressed.

As Paul writes, "Put on the new man who is renewed in knowledge according to the image of Him who created him" (Colossians 3:10). The new man is not fabricated—it is already present. The call is to live from what already is.

Dietrich Bonhoeffer noted, "The saints are not the perfectly pious, but those who experience the forgiveness of sins."[56] Their sanctity comes not from flawless performance but from perfect position in Christ.

VI. THE DANGER OF IDENTITY AMNESIA

Perhaps the greatest challenge to living from union is forgetting it. The enemy's strategy has always been to attack identity. "If You are the Son of God..." (Matthew 4:3) was Satan's opening temptation to Jesus. It remains his chief tactic against believers.

The apostle Peter warns against this spiritual amnesia: "But he who lacks these things is shortsighted, even to blindness, and has forgotten that he was cleansed from his old sins" (2 Peter 1:9). The root of spiritual stagnation is not lack of effort but lack of awareness—forgetting who we are in Christ.

When we forget who we are in Christ, we revert to religious striving, self-justification, and spiritual exhaustion. But when we remember—when we live from union—everything changes.

Theologian Rankin Wilbourne writes, "Union with Christ means that you're not defined by your past failures or your present struggles. You're defined by Christ's love for you and his life in you."[57] This truth must be continually reaffirmed in the believer's consciousness.

James calls the Word of God a mirror (James 1:23-25). It does not show us what to become, but who we already are. The challenge is not to improve ourselves, but to remain in the truth. "Let the word of Christ dwell in you richly" (Colossians 3:16). Identity, once grounded in Christ, becomes the anchor of the soul.

VII. THE HISTORICAL WITNESS TO UNION WITH CHRIST

The doctrine of union with Christ is not a modern innovation but a rediscovery of ancient truth. Throughout church history, the greatest teachers have recognized this reality as central to authentic Christian experience.

John Clayton, the Reformation theologian, placed extraordinary emphasis on union with Christ, writing, "We must understand that as long as Christ remains outside of us, and we are separated from him, all that he has suffered and done for the salvation of the human race remains useless and of no value for us."[58] For Clayton, union with Christ was not merely one doctrine among many but the sum of all spiritual blessings.

The Puritan John Owen devoted extensive writing to this theme, stating, "The first and principal grace is our union with Christ... This is that whereby the saints are really separated from the world and all cursed things therein, to the special favor of God."[59]

Even earlier, Bernard of Clairvaux wrote: "Jesus is honey in the mouth, melody in the ear, jubilation in the heart."[60]

This experiential knowledge of Christ's indwelling presence characterized the medieval mystics' understanding of union.

VIII. PRACTICAL IDENTITY FORMATION

Living from our identity in Christ requires intentional practices that reinforce this truth:

1. **Daily Identity Declarations**: Speaking Scripture over ourselves each morning, affirming who God says we are rather than what circumstances suggest.

2. **Community Reinforcement**: Surrounding ourselves with believers who speak identity rather than performance into our lives.

3. **Worship as Identity Expression**: Approaching worship not as earning God's pleasure but expressing our secure position as beloved children.

4. **Service from Overflow**: Engaging in ministry not to prove worth but to share the abundance we've already received.

Contemporary pastor and author Neil Anderson emphasizes, "What you do doesn't determine who you are; who you are determines what you do."[61] This fundamental shift from doing to being transforms every aspect of the Christian life.

CHAPTER 4

REST—THE FOUNDATION OF THE NEW CREATION LIFE

FROM STRIVING TO ABIDING IN THE FINISHED WORK

Rest is not the cessation of activity—it is the foundation of identity. In the kingdom of God, rest is not what happens after work is done; it is the divine position from which all spiritual life begins. From the beginning of the biblical story to the redemptive mission of Christ, rest is revealed as the birthplace of communion, authority, and true fruitfulness. In the New Covenant, rest is not merely a physical or emotional relief—it is a spiritual position rooted in union with Christ.

As Abraham Joshua Heschel beautifully expressed, "The Sabbath is not for the sake of the weekdays; the weekdays are for the sake of Sabbath. It is not an interlude but the climax of living."[62] This principle extends beyond the weekly Sabbath to the very nature of our life in Christ.

I. THE PATTERN OF REST IN CREATION

The first time Scripture mentions rest is in Genesis 2:2: "And on the seventh day God ended His work which He had done, and He rested." God did not rest because He was tired. He rested to delight in what was finished. The first full day of humanity's existence was a day of rest, not labor. Adam's life began not in toil, but in the enjoyment of God's presence.

The Book of Jubilees provides insight into early understanding of this pattern: "And He gave us a great sign, the Sabbath day, that we should work six days, but keep Sabbath on the seventh day from all work" (Jubilees 2:17). This text emphasizes that rest was built into creation's very structure.

This foundational truth is often missed: humanity was created from rest, not for rest. Work came after identity, not before it. In the Hebrew mindset, rest is not inactivity but a return to alignment with God's order. The Sabbath was instituted not merely as a ritual, but as a declaration that creation—and later, redemption—rests in the sufficiency of God, not the striving of man (Exodus 20:8-11).

Hebrews 4 connects this creation rest to the believer's spiritual life: "For we who have believed enter that rest" (Hebrews 4:3). In Christ, the believer returns to the original rhythm of divine design—work flowing from rest, not toward it.

As the Dead Sea Scrolls reflect in the Sabbath liturgy: "Blessed is He who created all things in perfect order and established a foundation of truth" (4Q403 1 i 32). Rest celebrates divine order, not human achievement.

II. JESUS'S INVITATION TO REST

Jesus affirms and fulfills the pattern of Sabbath rest in His invitation: "Come to Me, all you who labor and are heavy laden, and I will give you rest" (Matthew 11:28). This was not merely a call to weary workers. It was a radical declaration aimed at a generation crushed under religious burdens. The Pharisaic system had turned intimacy with God into performance for God. Jesus calls His hearers to unlearn striving and receive rest—not as a reward, but as a gift.

New Testament scholar Dale Bruner comments: "Jesus' invitation to rest is revolutionary because it comes not at the end of hard work but at the beginning of relationship with Him. Rest precedes and enables true service."[65]

He continues: "Take My yoke upon you and learn from Me... For My yoke is easy and My burden is light" (Matthew 11:29-30). The yoke was a rabbinic metaphor for a teacher's interpretation of Torah. Jesus, unlike the other teachers, invites us into a yoke that is light because it is not driven by fear, merit, or ritual obligation—it is governed by grace and secured by union.

This rest is not theoretical. It is relational. It is life flowing from the revelation that all striving to earn God's acceptance is ended at the cross. As Hebrews declares, "He who has entered His rest has himself also ceased from his works as God did from His" (Hebrews 4:10).

III. REST AS THE FRUIT OF UNION

Rest is the natural result of union with Christ. It is the soul's exhale when it discovers it is no longer on trial. When the believer sees that righteousness has already been imputed (Romans 4:6), that sonship has already been granted (Galatians 4:6-7), and that the Spirit already dwells within (Romans 8:9), rest becomes the default setting of the heart.

Theologian Michael Horton explains: "Rest is not the absence of activity but the absence of anxiety about our standing before God. It is the peace that comes from knowing our acceptance is secured in Christ, not achieved by us."[66]

This kind of rest is not passive. It is not indifference or apathy. It is active trust in the sufficiency of Christ. The believer does not rest because there is nothing to do, but because the most important thing has already been done. "It is finished" (John 19:30) is not the end of Jesus's work—it is the beginning of ours, now rooted in His completed victory.

Union with Christ means we no longer work for righteousness—we work from righteousness. We no longer strive to earn God's nearness—we live from the nearness He has already established by His Spirit. "You are not in the flesh but in the Spirit, if indeed the Spirit of God dwells in you" (Romans 8:9).

IV. REST VERSUS RELIGION

One of the most subtle enemies of spiritual rest is religion. While often intended to draw people to God, religious systems can unintentionally reinforce a merit-based mentality that contradicts the gospel. When external behaviors are emphasized over internal identity, rest is displaced by performance.

Paul confronted this repeatedly. To the Galatians, he wrote, "Are you so foolish? Having begun in the Spirit, are you now being made perfect by the flesh?" (Galatians 3:3). The danger wasn't just legalism—it was abandoning rest. The Galatians had started from union but were drifting back into effort.

Scholar Douglas Moo notes: "Paul's concern in Galatians is not merely theological but pastoral. He sees that returning to law-keeping destroys the rest and freedom that come from being in Christ."[67]

To the Colossians, he warned, "Let no one judge you... regarding a festival or a new moon or sabbaths... but the substance is of Christ" (Colossians 2:16-17). External forms cannot produce internal rest. Only Christ can.

Jesus Himself rebuked the Pharisees, who turned Sabbath into burden rather than blessing. "The Sabbath was made for man, and not man for the Sabbath" (Mark 2:27). In other words, rest is not a duty—it is a divine gift, a space where the soul returns to dependence on God.

V. PRACTICAL EXPRESSIONS OF REST

Living from rest has real implications. It transforms not only how we pray, serve, and worship—but how we think, feel, and decide. Rest affects our posture in every area of life. Here are a few practical outworkings:

- **Prayer becomes communion, not performance.** We stop begging and start listening. We shift from petitioning for acceptance to enjoying already-granted access (Hebrews 4:16).

- **Service becomes overflow, not obligation.** We no longer minister out of guilt, but out of joy. Ministry is no longer about earning favor—it is the fruit of abiding (John 15:5).

- **Worship becomes delight, not duty.** We cease performing songs to reach God and begin expressing love from already being in Him (John 4:23).

- **Decision-making becomes peaceful, not pressured.** We trust the indwelling Spirit, not our flesh-driven urgency (Romans 8:14).

- **Spiritual warfare becomes standing, not striving.** We fight from victory, not for it (Ephesians 6:13).

As Ruth Haley Barton observes: "Sabbath rest is more than mere cessation from work; it is an invitation to deeper communion with God that transforms how we approach all of life."[68]

This kind of rest produces fruit that striving cannot. Love, joy, peace, patience—all are fruit of the Spirit (Galatians 5:22-23), not achievements of effort. They manifest naturally when we live from union.

VI. GUARDING THE PLACE OF REST

Rest must be protected. Hebrews 4:11 exhorts, "Let us therefore be diligent to enter that rest." The paradox is intentional—rest is not effort, but it requires vigilance. The greatest threat to rest is unbelief. When we doubt God's Word or forget our identity, we slip back into striving.

Contemporary author John Eldredge writes: "The greatest threat to the Christian life is not outright sin but the slow drift from dependent rest into independent striving."[69]

David prayed, "Return to your rest, O my soul, for the LORD has dealt bountifully with you" (Psalm 116:7). This is a daily decision: to remind the soul of grace, to return to the truth of union, and to rest in what Christ has already accomplished.

Rest does not eliminate spiritual disciplines—it reorients them. Instead of becoming tools for performance, they become means of encounter. Instead of working for favor, we worship from fullness.

When believers learn to live from rest, they rediscover the power and simplicity of the gospel. The Christian life is no longer a struggle to reach God—it is a life of being carried by God. "In returning and rest you shall be saved; in quietness and confidence shall be your strength" (Isaiah 30:15).

VII. REST IN HISTORICAL CHRISTIAN THOUGHT

Throughout church history, various spiritual traditions have emphasized this principle of rest, though using different language:

The Desert Fathers spoke of "hesychia" (stillness) as essential to spiritual life. Evagrius Ponticus wrote: "When the soul has put away all distractions and returned to stillness, then it sees God clearly."[70]

The medieval mystics, like Meister Eckhart, taught: "God is not found in multiplicity, but in rest and unity. The soul finds God when it stops all activity and simply rests in His presence."[71]

The Puritan tradition, often mischaracterized as purely work-oriented, actually emphasized spiritual rest. Richard Sibbes wrote: "Rest in Christ, and let Him work in you, and for you, and through you."[72]

VIII. THE ESCHATOLOGICAL DIMENSION OF REST

Our present rest in Christ points toward an ultimate rest. As Hebrews 4:9-10 declares, "There remains therefore a rest for the people of God." This eternal Sabbath is not merely cessation from labor but the fullness of communion with God.

Theologian Jürgen Moltmann writes: "The Sabbath rest is a foretaste of the new creation, when God's presence will be fully manifest and all creation will rest in Him."[73]

CHAPTER 5

MANIFESTATION VERSUS ACQUISITION

LIVING FROM FULLNESS, NOT LACK

The difference between manifestation and acquisition is central to understanding the believer's life in Christ. Most religious systems are rooted in acquisition—do more to become more. But the gospel of Jesus Christ proclaims something radically different: that in union with Christ, we have already received all that pertains to life and godliness (2 Peter 1:3). The spiritual journey is not a pursuit of what we lack but a revelation of what we already possess. We are not climbing toward a higher status—we are awakening to the fullness already within us.

The language of Scripture consistently reflects this distinction. Believers are not called to *gain* righteousness, peace, or the presence of God—they are called to *walk* in them. The difference is not semantic—it is transformational.

As Watchman Nee powerfully expressed: "Christianity begins not with a big DO, but with a big DONE. The Christian life is not a matter of achieving but of receiving what has already been achieved."[74]

I. THE FINISHED WORK OF CHRIST

The starting point for manifestation is the finished work of Jesus. On the cross, Jesus declared, "It is finished" (John 19:30). This was not poetic closure—it was a legal, spiritual, and cosmic declaration that all that was required to restore humanity to union with God had been accomplished.

The Greek word used is "tetelestai," which literally means "paid in full." It was used in commercial transactions to indicate that a debt had been completely satisfied.[75] In the spiritual realm, it means that nothing is lacking in Christ's redemptive work.

Paul echoes this in Colossians 2:10: "You are complete in Him, who is the head of all principality and power." The believer's status is not partial, pending, or probationary—it is complete. This completeness is not based on performance but on position. The righteousness that believers manifest is not self-generated; it is received through Christ. "For He made Him who knew no sin to be sin for us, that we might become the righteousness of God in Him" (2 Corinthians 5:21).

This righteousness is not added to the believer incrementally; it is imparted fully at conversion. What remains is not acquisition but alignment—the process of allowing what is true in the spirit to be manifested in the soul and body.

II. ABIDING AND FRUITFULNESS

Jesus used the metaphor of a vine and branches to explain this principle: "Abide in Me, and I in you. As the branch cannot bear fruit of itself... neither can you unless you abide in Me" (John 15:4). The branch does not labor to acquire nutrients or force fruit into existence. It simply abides, and the life of the vine naturally flows through it.

Andrew Murray, in his classic work "Abide in Christ," writes: "The branch teaches a double lesson: doing nothing, and in doing nothing receiving all. The branch is manifestly limited to receiving what the vine gives."[76]

The believer, joined to Christ, is not trying to become fruitful—he or she is abiding in the One who is fruitful. "He who abides in Me, and I in him, bears much fruit" (John 15:5). The fruit of the Spirit—love, joy, peace, patience, kindness, and so on—are not goals to be achieved. They are manifestations of Christ's life within us (Galatians 5:22-23).

Attempting to acquire spiritual fruit by will power leads to frustration. But when believers live from their union with Christ, fruit emerges naturally. Paul affirms, "Christ lives in me" (Galatians 2:20). The indwelling Christ is not dormant—He is active, forming His nature in the believer (Galatians 4:19).

III. THE MISUNDERSTANDING OF "BECOMING"

Much of modern Christianity is filled with language about "becoming" more holy, more righteous, more spiritual. While well-intentioned, this language can reinforce a sense of deficiency rather than identity. The New Testament speaks less about becoming and more about being. Believers are "saints" (1 Corinthians 1:2), "new creations" (2 Corinthians 5:17), "children of God" (Romans 8:16), "partakers of the divine nature" (2 Peter 1:4), and "temples of the Holy Spirit" (1 Corinthians 6:19).

Theologian Thomas F. Torrance observed: "We are not working toward our justification but from it. We are not striving to become God's children but living as those who already are."[77]

This is not to deny that transformation occurs—but transformation is not a process of acquiring something we lack.

It is the unveiling of what is already true. Paul says, "Work out your own salvation with fear and trembling; for it is God who works in you" (Philippians 2:12-13). Note the order: what is *in* must be *worked out*. The believer does not work *for salvation* but *from* it.

The idea of "becoming" can subtly suggest distance from God. But Scripture teaches nearness: "The word is near you, in your mouth and in your heart" (Romans 10:8). The believer is not a seeker trying to reach God; he is a temple in whom God already dwells (2 Corinthians 6:16).

IV. LIVING FROM SUPPLY, NOT DEMAND

The law system operates on demand—"You shall, you must, you ought." But grace operates on supply—"God has, God gives, God empowers." The shift from law to grace is a shift from trying to meet God's requirements to trusting in God's provision.

Paul contrasts the two covenants in 2 Corinthians 3. The old covenant "kills," but the new covenant "gives life" (v. 6). Why? Because the law exposes lack, while the Spirit supplies abundance. When believers focus on demand, they live# Perfect Union: Living From Christ, Not For Him

CHAPTER 6

RENEWING THE MIND TO UNION REALITY

RECLAIMING OUR AWARENESS OF WHAT IS ALREADY TRUE

The human mind is the battleground of transformation. It is the place where truth must be remembered, error must be replaced, and the reality of our union with Christ must be continually affirmed. Though the believer's spirit is united with Christ at the moment of salvation (1 Corinthians 6:17), the experience of that union in daily life depends largely on the condition of the mind. The renewing of the mind is not about self-improvement; it is about alignment—bringing our thoughts into agreement with the finished work of Christ and the indwelling presence of the Holy Spirit.

Paul writes, "Do not be conformed to this world, but be transformed by the renewing of your mind" (Romans 12:2). Transformation is not the product of willpower but of revelation. The more clearly we see our identity in Christ, the more naturally we manifest His life.

As Dallas Willard observed: "The renovation of the heart is fundamentally a renovation of the mind—of the thought life. As we think, so we become."[85]

I. THE MIND AS THE INTERFACE BETWEEN SPIRIT AND BEHAVIOR

Human beings are triune in structure: spirit, soul, and body (1 Thessalonians 5:23). The spirit is where Christ now dwells by His Spirit. The body is the visible expression of life. But the mind—within the soul—is the bridge between the two. If the mind remains unrenewed, the truth in the spirit remains hidden. But if the mind is transformed, the reality within begins to manifest without.

Theologian Watchman Nee explains this tripartite nature: "The spirit is where we contact God, the soul is where we express our personality, and the body is where we contact the physical world. Renewal happens as the soul comes under the governance of the spirit."[86]

Paul describes this dynamic in Ephesians 4:22-24: "Put off... the old man... be renewed in the spirit of your mind, and... put on the new man." Notice: the new man is already present, but it must be "put on" through the renewal of the mind. Renewal is not creating something new—it is rediscovering and aligning with what already is.

II. THE DANGER OF A DOUBLE MIND

James warns, "A double-minded man is unstable in all his ways" (James 1:8). Double-mindedness occurs when the mind vacillates between spirit-truth and flesh-based perception. On one hand, we believe Christ dwells in us; on the other, we live as though we are distant from Him. This inner conflict creates spiritual instability and confusion.

The remedy is found in 2 Corinthians 10:4-5: "The weapons of our warfare are not carnal but mighty in God... bringing every thought into captivity to the obedience of Christ." The battlefield is mental, and the weapon is truth. Every thought that contradicts the believer's identity in Christ must be taken captive—not entertained, not analyzed, but cast down.

Psychologist and author Dr. Caroline Leaf notes: "Our thoughts literally shape our brain structure. What we meditate on creates neural pathways that either reinforce truth or error."[87]

When the mind is renewed, stability replaces doubt. The believer begins to walk in confidence, not because they feel spiritual, but because they know the truth. Jesus said, "You shall know the truth, and the truth shall make you free" (John 8:32). The implication is profound: bondage exists where truth is forgotten.

III. SCRIPTURE AS THE MIRROR OF UNION

James likens the Word of God to a mirror: "For if anyone is a hearer of the word and not a doer, he is like a man observing his natural face in a mirror... but forgets what kind of man he was" (James 1:23-24). The mirror reveals identity. The problem is not that believers do not have union—it is that they forget.

Biblical scholar Scot McKnight writes: "The Bible is not primarily a book of rules but a mirror in which we see who God is and who we are in relationship to Him. Transformation happens as we align our self-perception with God's perception of us."[88]

The mirror does not show us what to become—it shows us who we already are in Christ. The discipline of daily meditation on Scripture is not about religious duty; it is about anchoring the mind in identity. "Let the word of Christ dwell in you richly" (Colossians 3:16). When the Word governs the mind, union becomes not just doctrine—it becomes experience.

Psalm 1 describes the one who delights in God's Word as like a tree planted by rivers of water, bearing fruit in season (Psalm 1:2-3). This is not a picture of striving but of rootedness. The mind that meditates on truth becomes fertile ground for the Spirit to manifest Christ's life.

IV. FROM "BECOMING" TO "BEING" LANGUAGE

Renewing the mind also involves language. Many believers unknowingly reinforce old paradigms by how they speak: "I'm trying to become more loving... I need to become holy... I want to get closer to God." While sincere, such phrases betray a subtle denial of union. The truth is: the believer is already united with Christ, already indwelt by love, already holy in spirit (Hebrews 10:10).

Cognitive linguist George Lakoff has shown how language shapes thought patterns: "The words we use create mental frames that influence how we perceive reality. Changing our language can literally change our thinking."[89]

Paul writes, "Let the weak say, 'I am strong'" (Joel 3:10, quoted as a principle). Faith-filled language aligns with spiritual truth, not circumstantial perception. As Proverbs 18:21 reminds us, "Death and life are in the power of the tongue." The more believers speak as new creations, the more they think as new creations—and the more they live like it.

This is not positive thinking—it is faith speaking. Faith does not deny facts; it confesses truth. Abraham "did not waver at the promise of God through unbelief, but was strengthened in faith... and being fully convinced that what He had promised He was also able to perform" (Romans 4:20-21). Renewing the mind involves rehearsing what God has said, not what feelings or failures suggest.

V. PRACTICING THE PRESENCE OF CHRIST

One of the most effective ways to renew the mind is to practice the awareness of Christ's indwelling presence. Brother Lawrence, a 17th-century kitchen monk, referred to this as "the practice of the presence of God." While not a theologian in the formal sense, his simple discipline aligns perfectly with the truths of Scripture: "I am with you always" (Matthew 28:20), "Christ in you, the hope of glory" (Colossians 1:27), "The Spirit of God dwells in you" (Romans 8:9).

Modern neuroscience confirms what spiritual practitioners have long known: focused attention literally rewires the brain. Dr. Andrew Newberg's research on contemplative practice shows that regular meditation on spiritual truths creates lasting changes in brain structure.[90]

Renewal happens when the mind shifts from visiting God to dwelling with Him. Believers are not meant to "enter" God's presence occasionally—they are temples of His presence permanently (1 Corinthians 3:16). This awareness changes everything: temptation loses power, fear loses ground, and joy becomes constant.

Practices such as stillness, silence, breath prayers, and Scripture meditation help create space for this awareness. But the goal is not technique—it is connection. As Isaiah wrote, "You will keep him in perfect peace, whose mind is stayed on You" (Isaiah 26:3).

VI. RENEWAL IN COMMUNITY

The renewal of the mind is not only personal—it is communal. The early believers "continued steadfastly in the apostles' doctrine and fellowship" (Acts 2:42). Their minds were renewed together. Paul exhorted the Colossians to "admonish one another" with the Word (Colossians 3:16). Renewal thrives in environments where truth is spoken consistently and lovingly.

Social psychologist Nicholas Christakis has demonstrated how behaviors and beliefs spread through social networks: "We are influenced not just by our direct connections but by the connections of our connections. Renewal happens best in renewed communities."[91]

When believers gather not merely for instruction but for identity affirmation, their minds are fortified. Small groups, Bible studies, and corporate worship become spaces of renewal when rooted in the reality of union. "Encourage one another daily... so that none of you may be hardened by sin's deceitfulness" (Hebrews 3:13).

Community becomes a mirror as well—reminding one another of who we are in Christ when we forget. "As iron sharpens iron, so one person sharpens another" (Proverbs 27:17).

VII. NEURAL PATHWAYS AND SPIRITUAL TRUTH

Contemporary neuroscience offers fascinating insights into the renewal process. The brain's neuroplasticity means that new thought patterns create new neural pathways. When we consistently meditate on our identity in Christ, we literally rewire our brains to align with spiritual reality.

Dr. Caroline Leaf explains: "When you think, you build thoughts, and these become physical substances in your brain. Repetitive thinking patterns create default neural pathways. This is why Paul emphasizes thinking on whatever is true, noble, right, and pure (Philippians 4:8)."[92]

This scientific understanding reinforces the biblical principle: we are transformed by the renewing of our minds. Each time we choose to focus on our union with Christ rather than our circumstances, we strengthen the neural pathways of faith.

VIII. PRACTICAL TOOLS FOR MIND RENEWAL

1. **Identity Cards**: Create cards with identity scriptures to read daily.

2. **Thought Journals**: Track negative thoughts and replace them with truth.

3. **Meditation Apps**: Use technology to support regular Scripture meditation.

4. **Worship Playlists**: Curate music that reinforces identity truths.

5. **Accountability Partners**: Share your renewal journey with trusted friends.

6. **Truth Declarations**: Speak identity truths aloud each morning.

7. **Visual Reminders**: Place Scripture around your living space.

Contemporary teacher Graham Cooke emphasizes: "The biggest battle is in your thought life. Win the battle of the mind, and you'll win the battle of life. Think from your position in Christ, not toward it."[93]

IX. THE ROLE OF THE HOLY SPIRIT IN RENEWAL

While we participate in renewal through spiritual disciplines, the Holy Spirit is the ultimate agent of transformation. Jesus promised that the Spirit would "guide you into all truth" (John 16:13). The Spirit takes the objective truth of Scripture and makes it subjectively real in our experience.

Theologian Gordon Fee writes: "The Spirit's role is to make the reality of Christ's indwelling presence experientially real to the believer. He translates theological truth into lived experience."[94]

The Spirit also intercedes when our minds struggle to grasp truth: "The Spirit also helps in our weaknesses. For we do not know what we should pray for as we ought, but the Spirit Himself makes intercession for us" (Romans 8:26).

CHAPTER 7
EXPERIENCING UNION THROUGH CONTEMPLATIVE PRACTICE

AWAKENING TO WHAT IS ALREADY WITHIN

Union with Christ is not merely a doctrine to believe; it is a reality to experience. While the truth of our union is established at the moment of salvation—spiritually complete and unchangeable—our awareness of this union can grow deeper over time. Experiencing this union is not about achieving something new, but about becoming more awake to what has already been accomplished through the finished work of Christ. This chapter explores how contemplative practices, rooted in Scripture and modeled by Christ Himself, create space for our souls to perceive the presence that already abides within us.

As Thomas Merton wrote: "Contemplation is the highest expression of man's intellectual and spiritual life. It is that life itself, fully awake, fully active, fully aware that it is alive."[95]

I. EXPERIENTIAL UNION IN THE LIFE OF JESUS

Jesus modeled union not only in theology but in lived communion with the Father. He often withdrew to "lonely places" (Luke 5:16) or went up "on the mountain by Himself to pray" (Matthew 14:23). These were not acts of obligation, but of intimacy. Jesus, though sinless and filled with the Spirit, chose to retreat not for power but for presence—to remain relationally attuned to the One who sent Him.

Biblical scholar Darrell Bock notes: "Jesus' prayer life wasn't about obtaining something He lacked but about maintaining the conscious connection to the Father that characterized His entire ministry."[96]

In John 5:19, He said, "The Son can do nothing of Himself, but what He sees the Father do." His clarity of purpose, confidence in ministry, and stability in suffering flowed from a life of constant spiritual awareness. Though He was never separated from the Father, He cultivated an attentiveness that revealed what union looks like when it is actively perceived.

This rhythm of withdrawal and return—of silence, solitude, and stillness—is not an ancient relic but a present necessity. It is in these spaces that we learn not how to "get closer" to God, but how to become more conscious of His nearness.

II. THE BIBLICAL CALL TO STILLNESS AND MEDITATION

The Scriptures are filled with calls to contemplative stillness. "Be still, and know that I am God" (Psalm 46:10) is not a call to inactivity but to receptivity. The Hebrew word translated "be still" *(raphah)* means to release, relax, or let go. It is a command to cease striving and surrender into the awareness of God's sovereignty and presence.[97]

Isaiah echoes this in saying, "In returning and rest you shall be saved; in quietness and confidence shall be your strength" (Isaiah 30:15). The posture of inner stillness is not weakness—it is spiritual strength. Likewise, David speaks of "waiting silently for God alone" (Psalm 62:5) and of meditating "on [His] word day and night" (Psalm 1:2).

Old Testament scholar Walter Brueggemann observes: "The Psalms teach us that silence before God is not empty space but space filled with divine presence. It's where we learn to listen rather than speak, receive rather than demand."[98]

Paul exhorts believers to "set your minds on things above" (Colossians 3:2) and to "pray without ceasing" (1 Thessalonians 5:17). These are not mere intellectual activities—they are sustained attentions to the reality of Christ's indwelling presence.

III. PRACTICING THE PRESENCE OF GOD

The phrase "practicing the presence" gained popularity through the writings of Brother Lawrence, but the concept is deeply scriptural. The practice is simple: an intentional, moment-by-moment awareness of God's indwelling. "I am with you always" (Matthew 28:20), Jesus said. Paul confirmed, "Do you not know that Jesus Christ is in you?" (2 Corinthians 13:5). The goal of contemplative practice is not to invite God to come near—it is to attune our hearts to the reality that He is already here.

Contemporary contemplative Richard Rohr writes: "We cannot attain the presence of God because we're already totally in the presence of God. What's absent is awareness."[99]

This is not an esoteric or mystical idea. It is profoundly practical. It means doing the dishes with awareness of Christ's joy. It means walking into meetings with a sense of Christ's peace. It means waking up with gratitude and going to sleep with surrender. Practicing the presence transforms ordinary moments into holy encounters.

Paul teaches, "In Him we live and move and have our being" (Acts 17:28). The goal is not to compartmentalize spiritual experience but to dissolve the illusion of separation. Every breath becomes a prayer. Every task becomes worship. Every conversation becomes an opportunity for Christ to be manifested.

IV. SCRIPTURAL CONTEMPLATION (LECTIO DIVINA)

One powerful way to experience union is through meditative reading of Scripture. Known historically as *lectio divina* (divine reading), this practice moves beyond study to encounter. It involves four movements:

1. Lectio (Reading) – Slowly read a short passage of Scripture, allowing it to speak.

2. Meditatio (Meditation) – Reflect on a word or phrase that stands out, listening for what God is highlighting.

3. Oratio (Prayer) – Respond to God in prayer, letting your heart express what has surfaced.

4. Contemplatio (Contemplation) – Rest in silence, allowing God to speak and move beyond words.

While not prescribed by Scripture as a formula, these movements mirror biblical practice. Mary "pondered these things in her heart" (Luke 2:19). David said, "I will meditate on Your precepts" (Psalm 119:15). Meditation is not mind-emptying; it is Christ-filling.

Scholar Michael Casey explains: "Lectio divina is not about information but transformation. It's a way of allowing Scripture to read us, to penetrate beyond our intellectual defenses into the depths of our being."[100]

Scriptural contemplation grounds the soul in truth. It allows the Word to descend from intellect to spirit, from concept to communion.

V. SILENCE, SOLITUDE, AND SACRED STILLNESS

In a world of constant noise, silence becomes a prophetic act. Jesus "often withdrew" (Luke 5:16), not because He needed to escape, but because He prioritized presence. Solitude is not abandonment—it is invitation. It creates space for our fragmented souls to return to center.

Henri Nouwen writes: "Silence is the home of the word. Silence gives us a new eye to see and a new ear to hear. In silence, we can hear the voice that calls us the beloved."[101]

Elijah did not hear God in the wind, fire, or earthquake— but in a "still small voice" (1 Kings 19:12). The Spirit often speaks in whispers, not because He is weak, but because He is near. Stillness does not summon Him—it unveils Him.

Isaiah prophesies, "Your ears shall hear a word behind you, saying, 'This is the way, walk in it'" (Isaiah 30:21). Such sensitivity comes not from frenzy but from quiet communion. Jesus said, "My sheep hear My voice" (John 10:27). The practice of stillness refines our hearing and deepens our trust.

VI. UNION EXPERIENCED IN THE SACRAMENTAL AND THE ORDINARY

Contemplative union is not limited to silent prayer or Scripture meditation—it includes the sacraments and the sacredness of the ordinary. Communion, for example, is not mere symbolism. Paul writes, "The cup of blessing which we bless, is it not the communion of the blood of Christ?" (1 Corinthians 10:16). The Greek word *koinonia* (communion) means sharing, participation, fellowship. In the breaking of bread, we experience not merely remembrance but fellowship with the risen Christ.

Alexander Schmemann, Orthodox theologian, wrote: "The Eucharist is not a 'means of grace' but the manifestation of the Church as the body of Christ. In it, we don't just remember Christ; we participate in His life."[102]

Likewise, baptism is a participation in Christ's death and resurrection (Romans 6:3-5). These acts are not magical—they are material signs of spiritual realities, affirming the union that undergirds all Christian life.

Even in daily routines—eating, walking, resting—we can behold union. Paul writes, "Whatever you do, do all to the glory of God" (1 Corinthians 10:31). The goal is not to escape the world to find Christ—it is to recognize that Christ is present in all of life.

VII. CONTEMPLATIVE PRAYER FORMS

Various forms of contemplative prayer can help believers experience their union with Christ:

1. Centering Prayer: Choosing a sacred word as a symbol of consent to God's presence and action within.

2. Breath Prayer: Coordinating simple prayers with breathing (e.g., inhaling "Lord Jesus Christ," exhaling "have mercy on me").

3. Jesus Prayer: The ancient practice of repeating "Lord Jesus Christ, Son of God, have mercy on me, a sinner."

4. Welcoming Prayer: Embracing difficult emotions and circumstances as opportunities to consent to God's presence.

Cynthia Bourgeault explains: "Contemplative prayer is not about achieving a state but about surrendering to a relationship. It's how we learn to rest in the union that's already ours."[103]

VIII. MODERN NEUROSCIENCE AND CONTEMPLATION

Contemporary neuroscience is discovering what contemplatives have long known: sustained spiritual practice changes the brain. Dr. Andrew Newberg's research shows that contemplative prayer increases activity in the prefrontal cortex (associated with focus and compassion) while decreasing activity in the parietal lobe (associated with the sense of self).[104]

This scientific validation confirms the transformative power of contemplative practice. As we regularly focus on our union with Christ, our brains literally rewire to reflect this spiritual reality.

IX. OVERCOMING COMMON OBSTACLES

Many believers struggle with contemplative practice due to:

1. Distraction: The modern mind is conditioned for constant stimulation.

2. Guilt: Feeling that "doing nothing" is unproductive.

3. Impatience: Expecting immediate mystical experiences.

4. Fear: Worry about "emptying the mind" or engaging in "non-Christian" practices.

The key is understanding that Christian contemplation is not about emptying the mind but filling it with awareness of Christ's presence. It's not about achieving extraordinary experiences but attending to the extraordinary reality of union that's already ours.

Thomas Keating wisely noted: "Silence is God's first language; everything else is a poor translation. In order to hear that language, we must learn to be still and to rest in God."[105]

X. INTEGRATION INTO DAILY LIFE

The goal of contemplative practice is not to create spiritual specialists but to awaken ordinary believers to the extraordinary reality of union with Christ. As we develop these practices, we find that:

- Work becomes worship
- Relationships become sacramental
- Difficulties become opportunities for deeper trust
- Every moment becomes pregnant with divine presence

Brother Lawrence testified: "I cannot imagine how religious persons can live satisfied without the practice of the presence of God."[106]

As we cultivate contemplative awareness, we discover that union with Christ is not just a theological truth but an experiential reality that transforms every aspect of our lives.

CHAPTER 8

THE TRANSFORMATIVE POWER OF BEHOLDING

BECOMING BY GAZING, NOT STRIVING

The human soul is shaped by what it beholds. What captures our attention ultimately transforms our affections, our thinking, and our behavior. In the spiritual life, the single greatest agent of transformation is not discipline, duty, or religious obligation—it is beholding the glory of Christ. The Scripture proclaims, "But we all, with unveiled face, beholding as in a mirror the glory of the Lord, are being transformed into the same image from glory to glory" (2 Corinthians 3:18). This is not a poetic metaphor; it is a spiritual law: we become what we behold.

Beholding is the pathway to Christlikeness, and it is also the daily posture of one who is joined to Christ. It is not the work of the elite mystic or seasoned theologian—it is the calling of every believer. To behold is not to strain upward in spiritual ambition, but to open our inner eyes to the Christ who is already within (Colossians 1:27).

As A.W. Tozer profoundly stated: "What comes into our minds when we think about God is the most important thing about us... We tend by a secret law of the soul to move toward our mental image of God."[107]

I. BEHOLDING AND TRANSFORMATION IN SCRIPTURE

The biblical pattern is consistent: transformation flows not from effort but from vision. Moses spent forty days on Mount Sinai, beholding the glory of the Lord. When he descended, "the skin of his face shone" (Exodus 34:29). He did not try to become radiant—he simply reflected the One he gazed upon.

Old Testament scholar Terence Fretheim observes: "Moses' shining face was not the result of spiritual exercises but of prolonged exposure to God's presence. Transformation happens through encounter, not achievement."[108]

Isaiah saw the Lord "high and lifted up," and the vision of God's holiness caused him to see his own need for cleansing (Isaiah 6:1-7). The result was not despair but transformation— he was purified and commissioned. Ezekiel, too, fell on his face when beholding the glory of the Lord (Ezekiel 1:28), as did John in Revelation 1:17. Throughout the biblical narrative, encountering God's glory reorients the human soul.

The New Covenant deepens this reality. In Christ, believers are not only permitted to behold but are *invited* to gaze continually. "And we all... beholding... are being transformed" (2 Corinthians 3:18). This is not future hope—it is present reality. The transformation of the believer is not external conformity but internal unveiling.

II. CHRIST AS THE IMAGE WE BEHOLD

Colossians 1:15 declares that Christ "is the image of the invisible God." Hebrews 1:3 adds, "He is the radiance of the glory of God and the exact imprint of His nature." To behold

Christ, then, is to behold the perfect revelation of the Father. Jesus Himself said, "He who has seen Me has seen the Father" (John 14:9).

N.T. Wright explains: "Jesus is not just a window through which we see God; He is the perfect image in whom God is fully present and active. To behold Christ is to encounter God Himself."[109]

In the incarnation, Jesus became the visible display of divine character: mercy, justice, humility, authority, compassion, and power. But in the resurrection, He became more than a model— He became our very life. "When Christ who is our life appears, then you also will appear with Him in glory" (Colossians 3:4). Beholding Him is not merely admiring His virtue—it is awakening to the reality that His life is now our own.

Paul explains this mystery clearly: "Christ lives in me" (Galatians 2:20). The more we behold Him, the more the Spirit unveils that truth—not just intellectually but experientially. This is why Paul prays that "the eyes of your understanding be enlightened" (Ephesians 1:18). The eyes of the heart, not the mind, are where transformation begins.

III. BEHOLDING VERSUS BEHAVIOR MODIFICATION

One of the greatest errors in modern Christianity is the attempt to become like Christ through behavioral techniques alone. While discipline has its place, behavior modification apart from beholding always results in frustration. Moral striving without union leads to legalism, burnout, or hypocrisy.

John Piper emphasizes: "You don't become like Christ by trying to be like Christ. You become like Christ by looking at Christ. Beholding is becoming."[110]

Jesus did not say, "Try to act like Me." He said, "Abide in Me" (John 15:4). The fruit of the Spirit (Galatians 5:22-23) does not grow by effort, but by remaining connected to the vine. It is Christ's life, not the believer's effort, that produces lasting change.

This is why Paul focuses his letters not on outward behavior but inward identity. He tells the Corinthians to "behold as in a mirror" (2 Corinthians 3:18)—a reference to the Word of God and the revelation of Christ. The mirror shows who Christ is, and thus who we are in Him. As believers continually gaze upon Christ in the Word and in prayer, they begin to live from that unveiled identity.

IV. WAYS TO BEHOLD CHRIST

Beholding is not passive. It is intentional. It requires space, focus, and surrender. While there are many ways to behold Christ, the following practices have proven fruitful across generations:

- **Gospel Meditation** – Slowly reading the Gospels, not for information but for encounter. Picturing Jesus's compassion, listening to His voice, watching His actions—all while asking, "Lord, show me who You are in this moment."

Michael Card writes: "Biblical meditation is not emptying the mind but filling it with Christ. It's letting the Gospel narratives become living encounters."[111]

- **Worship in Spirit and Truth** – True worship is not performance—it is the heart's gaze fixed on the worth of Christ. "Worship the Lord in the beauty of holiness" (Psalm 96:9). In beholding Him, we become like Him.

- **Prayer as Presence** – Prayer is not simply petitions Through the Spirit, believers cry "Abba, Father!" (Romans 8:15), not as detached servants but as children united to God. The Spirit bears witness that we are children of God and "heirs—heirs of God and co-heirs with Christ" (Romans 8:17). This inheritance is not only future glory but present union.

The Spirit is the means by which we are sealed (Ephesians 1:13), sanctified (2 Thessalonians 2:13), and transformed (2 Corinthians 3:18). Union is not maintained by effort but by yielding to God's presence within.

Beholding Christ is not a religious ritual—it is relational intimacy. "Draw near to God and He will draw near to you" (James 4:8). But under the New Covenant, drawing near does not mean traveling far—it means awakening to the One already within.

V. THE MIRROR OF THE SPIRIT AND THE MIRROR OF THE WORD

2 Corinthians 3:18 speaks of beholding "as in a mirror." There are two mirrors the believer must use: the mirror of the Word and the mirror of the Spirit. The Word reveals Christ objectively; the Spirit unveils Him subjectively. One speaks to our understanding; the other to our spirit.

The Spirit does not contradict the Word—He illuminates it. Jesus said, "He will glorify Me, for He will take of what is Mine and declare it to you" (John 16:14). As we read the Word with the Spirit's help, we behold the Lord not as an idea, but as a present reality.

This mirrored beholding gradually transforms us "from glory to glory"—a process not of striving, but of unveiling. The veil of unbelief, fear, shame, and performance falls away, and we begin to see not only Christ clearly, but ourselves in Him.

VI. BECOMING WHAT WE BEHOLD

The biblical principle is consistent: we are transformed by what we consistently gaze upon. This is true in both directions. If we fixate on fear, we become anxious. If we obsess over sin, we become bound by it. But if we behold the Lamb of God, we are changed by Him.

Paul writes, "Set your mind on things above, not on things on the earth" (Colossians 3:2). He is not calling for escape from reality but for clarity about it. Christ is the true center of all things. To behold Him is to align with reality itself.

This transformation is not instantaneous, but it is inevitable. "The path of the righteous is like the light of dawn, shining brighter and brighter until full day" (Proverbs 4:18). As we behold Christ daily—in Word, worship, silence, and service— we become conformed to His image, not through pressure but through presence.

VII. HISTORICAL WITNESSES TO BEHOLDING

Throughout church history, various saints and mystics have emphasized the transformative power of beholding:

Gregory of Nyssa wrote: "What you gaze upon affects what you become. To behold God is to be progressively changed into His image."[112]

Teresa of Avila taught: "It is not by thinking much but by loving much that one draws nearest to God. Gaze upon Christ with the eyes of love."[113]

Julian of Norwich explained: "The highest form of prayer is to the goodness of God... We behold God and are beheld by Him. In this mutual beholding is our transformation."[114]

These voices, across different traditions and centuries, confirm the biblical pattern: we become what we behold.

VIII. THE PRACTICE OF BEHOLDING

Practical ways to cultivate the discipline of beholding:

1. Visual Meditation: Use Christian art and icons as windows to contemplate Christ's character.

2. Imaginative Prayer: Enter Gospel scenes through sanctified imagination, observing Jesus' actions and demeanor.

3. Nature Contemplation: See Christ's attributes reflected in creation (Romans 1:20).

4. Silence and Gazing: Spend time in wordless adoration, simply being present to the indwelling Christ.

5. Scriptural Gazing: Read passages slowly, pausing to visualize and internalize each truth about Christ.

Richard Foster advises: "In your devotional times, picture Jesus. If you cannot 'see' Him with your eyes, see Him with your heart. This is not vain imagination but faith in action."[115]

IX. BEHOLDING IN COMMUNITY

While beholding begins individually, it is enriched in community. As believers gather to worship, study, and share testimonies, they help each other see Christ more clearly.

Paul writes to the Philippians: "Join in following my example, and note those who so walk, as you have us for a pattern" (Philippians 3:17). We behold Christ not only directly but also as He is reflected in mature believers.

Small groups, spiritual friendships, and corporate worship all provide contexts where we can behold Christ together and be transformed collectively.

X. THE ULTIMATE BEHOLDING

Our present beholding, though transformative, is still partial. Paul acknowledges, "For now we see in a mirror, dimly, but then face to face" (1 Corinthians 13:12).

John gives us this promise: "Beloved, now we are children of God; and it has not yet been revealed what we shall be, but we know that when He is revealed, we shall be like Him, for we shall see Him as He is" (1 John 3:2).

The ultimate transformation comes through ultimate beholding. But even now, every glimpse of Christ's glory changes us. As we behold, we become. As we gaze, we are transformed. This is not the labor of religion but the leisure of love—not the strain of achievement but the surrender of attention.

Thomas à Kempis captured this beautifully: "Without Christ I can do nothing, with Christ I can do all things. When I behold Him, I am changed. When I gaze upon His beauty, I reflect His glory."[116]

CHAPTER 9

UNION IN COMMUNITY–THE CORPORATE EXPRESSION

WE ARE ONE BODY IN CHRIST

Union with Christ is not a private possession—it is a shared reality. While salvation is deeply personal, it is never solitary. Every believer who is joined to Christ is also joined to every other believer. Paul's language is emphatic: "For we, though many, are one body in Christ, and individually members of one another" (Romans 12:5). Union with Christ creates union among His people. The corporate nature of this union is not metaphorical—it is mystical, real, and functional.

As individual branches abide in the same vine, so every believer abides in Christ and therefore in relational connection to every other believer (John 15:5). This is why the New Testament so often speaks of the church as a *body*, a *temple*, a *household*, and a *bride*—images that emphasize both unity and interdependence.

Stanley Hauerwas observes: "The church does not have a social ethic; the church is a social ethic. Our life together in Christ is itself a witness to the world of what God has done."[117]

This chapter explores the communal implications of union with Christ—how we live, love, correct, and build one another up as those who are united not only to the Head but to each other.

I. THE BODY OF CHRIST AND THE SPIRIT OF UNITY

Paul writes, "For by one Spirit we were all baptized into one body—whether Jews or Greeks... and have all been made to drink into one Spirit" (1 Corinthians 12:13). The Holy Spirit does not merely connect us to Christ; He connects us to each other. Unity is not a goal to be achieved—it is a reality to be protected.

Theologian Miroslav Volf emphasizes: "The church's unity is not organizational but pneumatological—it's created and sustained by the Holy Spirit who indwells all believers and binds them to Christ and one another."[118]

Ephesians 4:3 urges believers to be "eager to maintain the unity of the Spirit in the bond of peace." Notice that unity is not something we create—it is something we maintain. The Spirit establishes our union; we are called to honor and express it.

This unity is not uniformity. The body of Christ includes diversity in personality, culture, gifting, and maturity. Yet it is a diversity united under one Head. Paul writes, "Now you are the body of Christ, and members individually" (1 Corinthians 12:27). Each member matters. Each contributes. And each is affected by the health—or sickness—of the whole.

II. LOVE AS THE CULTURE OF UNION

Jesus said, "By this all will know that you are My disciples, if you have love for one another" (John 13:35). Love is not the fruit of human niceness—it is the manifestation of divine union. As Jesus is in the Father and we are in Him, so we are called to love one another with the same selfless, sacrificial, and steadfast love.

Paul described this in detail: "Love suffers long and is kind... it does not envy... it is not puffed up... it bears all things, believes all things, hopes all things, endures all things" (1 Corinthians 13:4-7). This love is not natural. It flows from union.

Dietrich Bonhoeffer wrote: "Christian brotherhood is not an ideal which we must realize; it is rather a reality created by God in Christ in which we may participate."[119]

When the church walks in this love, it becomes a prophetic witness to the world—a living expression of Christ's body. As believers live in awareness of their shared union, they begin to see Christ in one another. The weak are lifted. The strong are humbled. The offended forgive. The offended are corrected. The community grows in holiness and wholeness.

III. ACCOUNTABILITY IN THE BODY OF CHRIST

Union does not remove responsibility—it deepens it. Because we are members of one another, we are accountable to one another. Hebrews 3:13 instructs, "Exhort one another daily... lest any of you be hardened through the deceitfulness of sin." This is not meddling—it is love.

Paul commands, "If anyone is caught in any transgression, you who are spiritual should restore him in a spirit of gentleness" (Galatians 6:1). The goal is always restoration, not condemnation. But love that ignores sin is not love—it is abandonment. James affirms this, saying, "Whoever turns a sinner from the error of his way will save a soul from death" (James 5:20).

Jesus outlined a process of correction in Matthew 18:15-17:

1. **Private Confrontation** – "Go and tell him his fault between you and him alone."

2. **Small Group Confirmation** – "If he will not hear, take with you one or two more."

3. **Community Involvement** – "If he refuses to hear them, tell it to the church."

4. **Exclusion if Necessary** – "If he refuses... let him be to you like a heathen and a tax collector."

This is not about rejection but repentance. The goal is not punishment—it is clarity. Sin that is tolerated within the body corrodes the community and dishonors the Head.

IV. THE ROLE OF CHURCH DISCIPLINE

Paul's instruction in 1 Corinthians 5 provides a sobering example of communal accountability. A man was engaging in sexual immorality "that is not even named among the Gentiles" (v. 1). The church had become arrogant rather than mournful. Paul responds, "Deliver such a one to Satan for the destruction of the flesh, that his spirit may be saved" (v. 5).

This is excommunication—removal from the fellowship of the body. It is not hatred but hope: that separation might bring conviction, and conviction might lead to repentance.

Later, Paul instructs the church to welcome the repentant man back, "lest perhaps such a one be swallowed up with too much sorrow" (2 Corinthians 2:7). The process of church discipline must always be guided by both holiness and compassion.

When a community tolerates unrepentant sin in the name of love, it ceases to be a prophetic witness. But when it exercises truth in love, discipline becomes a means of grace. Paul warns,

"A little leaven leavens the whole lump" (1 Corinthians 5:6). The purity of the body affects the health of all.

V. MUTUAL EDIFICATION AND SHARED IDENTITY

Beyond correction, union calls us to mutual edification. Paul commands, "Let all things be done for edification" (1 Corinthians 14:26). The gifts of the Spirit are given "for the profit of all" (1 Corinthians 12:7). Ministry is not performance—it is participation in the life of the body.

Each member has something to contribute. One brings a word. Another, a song. Another, discernment. Another, compassion. As each part does its work, "the whole body... grows and builds itself up in love" (Ephesians 4:16). Union creates not competition, but interdependence.

This is why isolation is so dangerous. A detached limb dies. A disconnected believer drifts. "Let us not give up meeting together... but encouraging one another" (Hebrews 10:25). Community is not optional for the believer—it is essential for the life of Christ to be expressed corporately.

VI. THE CHURCH AS THE MANIFESTATION OF CHRIST

The ultimate goal of union in community is not merely fellowship—it is incarnation. The church is not a club or a classroom. It is the living body of the risen Christ on earth. Paul writes, "The church... is His body, the fullness of Him who fills all in all" (Ephesians 1:22-23). The corporate church reveals Christ's presence in a way that no individual can alone.

Perfect Union

When the church lives from union—with Christ and one another—it becomes a sanctuary for the broken, a lighthouse for the lost, and a witness to the world. "By this shall all men know..." (John 13:35). Love is not merely the ethic of community—it is the expression of union.

VII. DIVERSITY WITHIN UNITY

The New Testament vision of the church emphasizes both unity and diversity. Paul uses the body metaphor to illustrate this: "For as the body is one and has many members, but all the members of that one body, being many, are one body, so also is Christ" (1 Corinthians 12:12).

Different gifts, backgrounds, and functions don't threaten unity—they express it. The eye cannot say to the hand, "I have no need of you" (1 Corinthians 12:21). Every member is necessary for the full expression of Christ's body.

This diversity-in-unity reflects the very nature of God and His redemptive plan. As Paul declares, "There is neither Jew nor Greek, there is neither slave nor free, there is neither male nor female; for you are all one in Christ Jesus" (Galatians 3:28).

VIII. THE MINISTRY OF RECONCILIATION

Because we are united in Christ, we become agents of reconciliation. Paul writes, "All this is from God, who reconciled us to himself through Christ and gave us the ministry of reconciliation" (2 Corinthians 5:18).

This reconciliation happens on multiple levels:

1. Between individuals and God

2. Between estranged believers

3. Between different cultural and ethnic groups

4. Between the church and the world

The church becomes a living demonstration of God's reconciling power, showing the world what restored relationships look like.

IX. CORPORATE SPIRITUAL PRACTICES

Union in community is nurtured through shared spiritual practices:

1. **Corporate Worship**: Gathering to exalt Christ together

2. **Communion**: Sharing in the Lord's Supper as one body

3. **Prayer**: Agreeing together in intercession

4. **Scripture Reading**: Hearing God's Word as a community

5. **Baptism**: Celebrating new believers' union with Christ

6. **Testimony**: Sharing stories of God's faithfulness

7. **Service**: Working together in ministry

These practices reinforce our corporate identity and strengthen the bonds of fellowship.

X. THE WITNESS OF UNITY

Jesus prayed for His followers, "that they may be one, even as we are one... so that the world may know that you sent me" (John 17:22-23). The unity of believers is itself an apologetic—a testimony to the reality of Christ.

Perfect Union

When the church demonstrates supernatural unity across natural divisions, it bears witness to the reconciling power of the gospel. This unity is not achieved through human effort but received as a gift of our union with Christ.

Francis Schaeffer called this "the final apologetic"—the love and unity of Christians as the ultimate proof of Christianity's truth. When believers live in the reality of their shared union with Christ, they become a compelling witness to a fractured world.

CHAPTER 10

UNION AND ASSIGNMENT—LIVING FROM CHRIST, NOT FOR A STAGE

Your Calling is Christ. Your Assignment is What Flows from Him.

In the modern church, few concepts have been more misunderstood than "calling." Often used to describe roles in ministry, platforms, or spiritual gifts, the term has come to mean almost anything a believer feels passionate about. But Scripture teaches something deeper and more foundational: our calling is not first to do something—it is to Someone. We are called into union with Christ. Every legitimate assignment flows from that place of communion.

Paul writes to the Corinthians, "God is faithful, by whom you were called into the fellowship of His Son, Jesus Christ our Lord" (1 Corinthians 1:9). That is our primary calling: fellowship—*koinonia*—participation in the life of Christ. It is not a role to perform but a relationship to abide in. From that eternal calling, temporal assignments are birthed.

Os Guinness clarifies: "Our primary calling as followers of Christ is by him, to him, and for him. Our secondary calling, considering God's purposes for us, is to do our work in the world."[120]

This chapter reclaims the distinction between calling and assignment. It shows how identity in Christ precedes all activity, and how confusion on this issue has produced burnout, celebrity Christianity, and misplaced ambition.

I. THE ETERNAL CALL: CHRIST HIMSELF

The Greek word for "calling" *(klesis)* appears repeatedly in the New Testament, and it most often refers to the believer's relationship to Christ—not to a job or ministry. Paul speaks of "the upward call of God in Christ Jesus" (Philippians 3:14), "the hope of His calling" (Ephesians 1:18), and being "called to be saints" (Romans 1:7).

Gordon Smith writes: "The language of call in Scripture is fundamentally about identity and relationship, not function or role. We are called to belong to Christ before we are called to do anything for Christ."[121]

Our call is to become one with Christ—to share His life, partake in His sufferings, and be conformed to His image (Romans 8:29). It is a call to *be,* not a call to *do.* Jesus did not say, "Follow your calling"; He said, "Follow Me" (Matthew 4:19).

When we make assignments our identity, we invert the order of the kingdom. Assignments are seasonal. They may shift. They may end. But our union with Christ is eternal and unchanging. The moment we tie our worth to what we do "for God," we have subtly departed from living in God.

II. ASSIGNMENT: THE EXPRESSION OF UNION

An assignment is the role or task given by God for a season or purpose. Paul writes, "We are His workmanship, created in Christ Jesus for good works, which God prepared beforehand that we should walk in them" (Ephesians 2:10). These good works are not our identity—they are our expression.

Frederick Buechner famously described vocation as "the place where your deep gladness and the world's deep hunger meet."[122] But this meeting point is discovered through union, not ambition.

Assignments vary: a mother raising children, a pastor shepherding a flock, an artist creating beauty, a businessman stewarding resources, a servant quietly praying in secret. But all share the same root—union. Jesus said, "I am the vine, you are the branches... he who abides in Me... bears much fruit" (John 15:5). The branch doesn't choose the kind of fruit—it simply abides and manifests what the vine supplies.

Assignments are not measured by visibility but by obedience. Jesus spent 30 years in obscurity and 3 in public ministry. Paul spent years in preparation before being released into apostolic labor. John the Baptist decreased so Christ could increase. The measure of success is not crowds but faithfulness.

III. THE DANGERS OF CONFUSING CALLING AND ASSIGNMENT

When believers confuse their calling (Christ) with their assignment (ministry), several distortions emerge:

- **Performance replaces intimacy**. Ministry becomes a way to earn approval instead of a response to abiding in grace.

- **Burnout replaces fruitfulness**. Instead of resting in Christ, believers strive to "make something happen," often at the expense of their soul.

- **Comparison replaces contentment**. Assignments are diverse. But when assignment is mistaken for identity, believers begin to compare and compete.

- **Platform replaces presence.** The desire for visibility overtakes the desire for communion. Social media exacerbates this, making ministry into branding rather than service.

- **When the assignment ends, the person collapses.** Retired pastors, failed leaders, and burned-out missionaries often experience crisis when their role is stripped. But if our identity is rooted in union, we remain secure regardless of title.

Henri Nouwen wrote about this from personal experience: "I am deeply convinced that the Christian leader of the future is called to be completely irrelevant and to stand in this world with nothing to offer but his or her own vulnerable self."[123]

Paul modeled this clarity. Though called as an apostle, he introduced himself foremost as "a bondservant of Jesus Christ" (Romans 1:1). His identity was not rooted in title but in belonging. Whether planting churches, making tents, or sitting in prison, his union with Christ defined him.

IV. ASSIGNMENTS FLOW FROM BEING, NOT DOING

Union with Christ reorients the entire framework of how we discern assignment. We no longer ask, "What am I called to do?" but "Who am I called to remain in?" From that abiding, fruit emerges.

Jesus Himself did nothing independently. He said, "The Son can do nothing of Himself... but what He sees the Father do" (John 5:19). Even His assignment—to proclaim the kingdom, heal the sick, and go to the cross—was executed from intimacy, not initiative. "I do not seek My own will but the will of the Father who sent Me" (John 5:30).

The same is true for us. Our assignment is not ours to invent. It is revealed through relationship, through prayerful attentiveness, through obedience in the mundane. God speaks to those who rest in Him.

Paul writes, "Whatever you do, do all in the name of the Lord Jesus" (Colossians 3:17). That includes the platform and the parking lot. There is no hierarchy of spiritual assignments— only a hierarchy of surrender.

V. DISCERNING YOUR ASSIGNMENT WITHOUT LOSING YOUR IDENTITY

How do we discern an assignment without losing sight of union?

1. **Start with Presence, Not Passion.** Passion alone can deceive. Presence is where clarity comes. "Delight yourself in the Lord, and He shall give you the desires of your heart" (Psalm 37:4).

2. **Listen for the Spirit's Leading.** "As many as are led by the Spirit of God, these are sons of God" (Romans 8:14).

3. **Be Faithful in the Small.** David tended sheep before slaying giants. Jesus washed feet before ascending the throne.

4. **Submit to Community.** The early church laid hands on those already faithful (Acts 13:1-3). The body confirms assignment through discernment.

5. Hold It Loosely. Paul planted churches but was not shaken when jailed. His joy was Christ (Philippians 3:8-10), not success.

Parker Palmer advises: "Before I can tell my life what I want to do with it, I must listen to my life telling me who I am."[124]

VI. RETURNING TO THE SIMPLICITY OF UNION

In 2 Corinthians 11:3, Paul expresses concern that believers might be "corrupted from the simplicity that is in Christ." That simplicity is union. The early believers were not obsessed with platforms or personal destinies—they were obsessed with Jesus. "They continued steadfastly in the apostles' doctrine and fellowship... breaking of bread and in prayers" (Acts 2:42). From that simplicity, the world was turned upside down.

Assignments matter. Ministry matters. But they must flow from the well of communion. Otherwise, they become idols. As Jesus warned in Matthew 7:22-23, there will be those who prophesied, cast out demons, and did "many wonders" in His name—and yet He will say, "I never knew you." The issue was not lack of fruit—it was lack of union.

VII. HISTORICAL EXAMPLES OF CALLING AND ASSIGNMENT

Throughout church history, many servants of God have demonstrated the proper relationship between calling and assignment:

Brother Lawrence served as a kitchen worker in a monastery, finding God equally present in washing dishes as in formal prayer. His assignment was mundane; his calling was profound.

Amy Carmichael went to India as a missionary but spent most of her life running an orphanage. Her assignment changed; her calling to Christ remained constant.

Corrie ten Boom was a watchmaker who became a Holocaust rescuer and later a traveling speaker. Her assignments varied dramatically; her identity in Christ stayed secure.

William Wilberforce was called to Christ and assigned to politics, spending decades fighting slavery. He understood his parliamentary work as an expression of his primary calling to God.

VIII. THE FREEDOM OF IDENTITY-BASED ASSIGNMENT

When we understand that our calling is to Christ and our assignments flow from Him, several freedoms emerge:

1. **Freedom from Performance Anxiety**: We don't have to prove our worth through our work.

2. **Freedom to Change**: Assignments can shift without threatening our identity.

3. **Freedom from Comparison**: Different assignments don't mean different values.

4. **Freedom to Rest**: We can cease from labor without ceasing from purpose.

5. **Freedom to Fail:** Failed assignments don't equal failed calling.

Eugene Peterson reflected: "The vocation of pastor has been replaced by the strategies of religious entrepreneurs with business plans."[125] When we return to calling as union with Christ, we escape this entrepreneurial trap.

IX. CORPORATE IMPLICATIONS

This understanding of calling and assignment has profound implications for church life:

1. **Leadership Selection**: We look for those who abide in Christ, not just those with impressive gifts.

2. **Ministry Evaluation**: We measure fruitfulness, not just productivity.

3. **Discipleship Focus**: We emphasize being with Jesus before doing for Jesus.

4. **Burnout Prevention**: We encourage rest and relationship, not just results.

5. **Transition Support**: We help people navigate assignment changes without identity crises.

X. LIVING THE INTEGRATED LIFE

Ultimately, the goal is integration—where calling and assignment flow together seamlessly. This happens when:

1. We remain rooted in our identity as beloved children

2. We listen attentively to the Spirit's guidance

3. We serve from overflow rather than obligation

4. We hold assignments lightly while clinging to Christ tightly

5. We measure success by faithfulness, not visibility

Thomas Merton wrote: "To say that I am made in the image of God is to say that love is the reason for my existence, for God is love. Love is my true identity. Selflessness is my true self. Love is my true character. Love is my name."[126]

When we understand that our deepest calling is to participate in the love of Christ, every assignment becomes an opportunity to express that love. We no longer live for a stage but from a union that transforms everything we do into worship.

CHAPTER 11
UNION AND SUFFERING—FINDING CHRIST IN LIFE'S CHALLENGES

GLORY HIDDEN IN AFFLICTION, CHRIST REVEALED IN TRIAL

Union with Christ does not insulate us from suffering—it transforms how we walk through it. For many believers, suffering is misunderstood as a sign of divine absence or judgment. But in the framework of union, suffering becomes a sacred context for deeper communion. It is not punishment, but participation; not distance from God, but often the space where Christ is most fully revealed.

Paul wrote, "That I may know Him... and the fellowship of His sufferings, being conformed to His death" (Philippians 3:10). This is not spiritual masochism—it is the cry of someone who understands that the crucible of trial reveals union in ways comfort never could. In suffering, the believer does not walk alone. Christ is there—not as a distant sympathizer, but as the indwelling Savior who shares in every wound.

Elisabeth Elliot, who experienced profound loss, wrote: "God never denies us our heart's desire except to give us something better."[127] This "something better" is often a deeper experience of Christ Himself.

I. SUFFERING IS NOT THE ABSENCE OF GOD

Throughout Scripture, those most deeply used by God endured profound suffering. Joseph was betrayed and imprisoned. David was hunted and falsely accused. Jeremiah was beaten and ridiculed. Paul was whipped, stoned, and shipwrecked. Even Jesus—sinless and perfect—was "a Man of sorrows and acquainted with grief" (Isaiah 53:3).

None of these stories indicate abandonment. Rather, they reveal a divine mystery: suffering is often the context in which the presence of God becomes most personal. As David confessed, "Even though I walk through the valley of the shadow of death, I will fear no evil; for You are with me" (Psalm 23:4).

The Hebrew word for "with" *(immadi)* suggests intimate accompaniment—literally "at my side."[128] God doesn't observe our suffering from heaven; He enters into it with us.

Union means Christ does not meet us *after* the storm— He is *in* the storm. He does not watch from afar—He lives within, weeping when we weep, strengthening us from within. "He Himself has said, 'I will never leave you nor forsake you'" (Hebrews 13:5).

II. SHARING IN THE FELLOWSHIP OF HIS SUFFERINGS

Paul's desire to "know Him... and the fellowship of His sufferings" (Philippians 3:10) seems paradoxical in a world obsessed with comfort. But Paul understood that suffering for Christ—or with Christ—was not to be feared. It was a door into deeper intimacy.

The Greek word for "fellowship" *(koinonia)* implies sharing, participation, and common experience.[129] We don't merely endure suffering; we share in Christ's own experience of it.

To share in Christ's sufferings is not to repeat His redemptive work—only He bore the sin of the world (1 Peter 2:24). But we are invited to participate in His life, and that includes His path of obedience through hardship. "Though He was a Son, yet He learned obedience by the things which He suffered" (Hebrews 5:8).

Biblical scholar Peter O'Brien explains: "Paul sees suffering not as evidence of God's displeasure but as a means of deeper conformity to Christ. It's through suffering that we experientially enter into the reality of our union with Him."[130]

In suffering, pride is crushed, idols are exposed, and self-sufficiency dies. We begin to echo Jesus in Gethsemane: "Not My will, but Yours be done" (Luke 22:42). This surrender is not loss—it is the unveiling of divine life. "For our light affliction... is working for us a far more exceeding and eternal weight of glory" (2 Corinthians 4:17).

III. UNION REFRAMES EVERY TRIAL

Without union, suffering feels like abandonment. With union, it becomes refinement. James writes, "Count it all joy when you fall into various trials, knowing that the testing of your faith produces patience" (James 1:2-3). Trials do not create faith—they reveal and refine it.

Peter affirms, "Though now for a little while... you have been grieved by various trials, that the genuineness of your faith... may be found to praise, honor, and glory at the revelation of Jesus Christ" (1 Peter 1:6-7). Trials become the stage for the revelation of Christ—not only to others, but to us.

The key insight is that trials "test" *(dokimion)* our faith—like fire tests gold, revealing its purity.[131] Suffering doesn't determine our value; it reveals what's already there.

Union assures us that suffering is never wasted. Whether it is the pain of betrayal, illness, persecution, or inner torment, every valley becomes a place of revelation. "He gives beauty for ashes, the oil of joy for mourning" (Isaiah 61:3).

IV. CHRIST IN US: THE HOPE IN AFFLICTION

The great hope in suffering is not that it will end quickly—but that Christ is in it. Paul writes from prison, "Christ in you, the hope of glory" (Colossians 1:27). This is not theory—it is testimony. From dark cells and chains, Paul sang hymns (Acts 16:25). From affliction, he wrote letters of joy (Philippians 4:4).

Christ in us means that we never suffer alone. It means comfort is not only external but internal. "The sufferings of Christ abound in us, so our consolation also abounds through Christ" (2 Corinthians 1:5). Comfort flows not from escape but from presence. God is not waiting at the finish line—He is walking with us each step of the way.

Amy Carmichael, who suffered chronic pain for the last twenty years of her ministry, wrote: "One can give without loving, but one cannot love without giving. The cross is the touchstone of love."[132]

V. MINISTERING FROM BROKENNESS

Union transforms suffering not only for us but through us. Those who suffer with Christ are entrusted with the ministry of

His comfort. Paul writes, "Blessed be... the God of all comfort, who comforts us... that we may be able to comfort those who are in any trouble" (2 Corinthians 1:3-4).

Wounded believers are not disqualified—they are often more qualified. Scars become testimonies. Weakness becomes a platform for God's strength. "My grace is sufficient for you, for My strength is made perfect in weakness" (2 Corinthians 12:9).

Henri Nouwen called this the "wounded healer" paradigm—those who minister from their own places of pain often carry the deepest authority.[133] The world doesn't need perfect Christians; it needs present ones.

The world does not need perfect Christians—it needs present ones. People who have walked through fire and come out carrying His fragrance. As Paul declared, "We are the fragrance of Christ... among those who are perishing" (2 Corinthians 2:15).

VI. FUTURE GLORY AND PRESENT ASSURANCE

Union sustains us not only in this life but in the hope of resurrection. Paul writes, "If we suffer with Him, we shall also be glorified together" (Romans 8:17). This is not merit-based reward but relational participation. Suffering with Christ now is part of the preparation for reigning with Him then.

He continues, "The sufferings of this present time are not worthy to be compared with the glory which shall be revealed in us" (Romans 8:18). Our union assures us that present pain is not the end of the story.

Until then, we groan, we hope, and we abide. Not as orphans, but as sons. Not in defeat, but in hidden glory. "Though our outward man is perishing, yet the inward man is being renewed day by day" (2 Corinthians 4:16).

VII. TYPES OF SUFFERING IN UNION

Union with Christ doesn't eliminate suffering but gives it meaning. Several types of suffering are transformed through union:

1. **Persecution for Faith**: "Blessed are you when they revile and persecute you...for My sake" (Matthew 5:11). This suffering confirms our identity.

2. **Consequences of Living in a Fallen World**: Illness, loss, natural disasters. These remind us that creation itself groans for redemption (Romans 8:22).

3. **Discipline from the Father**: "Whom the Lord loves He chastens" (Hebrews 12:6). This suffering refines us.

4. **Spiritual Warfare**: "We do not wrestle against flesh and blood" (Ephesians 6:12). This suffering reveals our authority in Christ.

5. **Sharing Others' Burdens**: "Bear one another's burdens, and so fulfill the law of Christ" (Galatians 6:2). This suffering expresses love.

VIII. HISTORICAL WITNESSES TO SUFFERING IN UNION

Throughout church history, saints have discovered Christ's presence in suffering:

John of the Cross wrote about the "dark night of the soul," where God purifies the believer through spiritual dryness. He taught that this darkness is actually union becoming deeper, though it feels like abandonment.[134]

Madame Guyon, imprisoned for her faith, wrote: "I have found that the darkness through which I have passed has been the means of bringing me into a marvelous light."[135]

Dietrich Bonhoeffer, facing execution, penned: "When Christ calls a man, he bids him come and die." Yet his prison letters radiate joy and hope.[136]

Corrie ten Boom, survivor of Nazi concentration camps, testified: "There is no pit so deep that God's love is not deeper still."[137]

IX. PRACTICAL RESPONSES TO SUFFERING

How do we live out union with Christ in suffering?

1. **Honest Lament**: The Psalms show us that honest expression of pain is not lack of faith. Jesus Himself quoted Psalm 22 on the cross.

2. **Active Surrender**: Not passive resignation but active yielding to God's purposes.

3. **Community Support**: Allowing others to "weep with those who weep" (Romans 12:15).

4. **Spiritual Disciplines**: Maintaining practices that anchor us in truth when feelings fail.

5. **Redemptive Perspective**: Looking for how God might use our pain for others' healing.

6. Hope in Resurrection: Remembering that present suffering is temporary; glory is eternal.

X. THE MYSTERY OF SUFFERING IN UNION

Ultimately, suffering in union with Christ remains a mystery. We don't always understand why God allows specific trials. But we trust Who is with us in them.

Paul learned through his "thorn in the flesh" that God's grace is sufficient (2 Corinthians 12:7-10). Sometimes the greatest miracle is not removal of suffering but the presence of Christ within it.

Elisabeth Elliot wrote: "God never uses anyone greatly until He has wounded him deeply."[138] This wounding is not punitive but preparatory. It creates capacity for both divine comfort and compassionate ministry.

The cross remains the ultimate paradigm. What looked like defeat became victory. What seemed like abandonment revealed love's deepest expression. In union with Christ, our sufferings participate in this same pattern of death and resurrection.

As we suffer with Christ, we discover what Paul knew: "I have been crucified with Christ; it is no longer I who live, but Christ lives in me" (Galatians 2:20). In our weakness, His strength is perfected. In our brokenness, His wholeness is revealed. In our dying, His life is manifested.

This is the paradox of union in suffering: we are never more alive than when we die with Christ, never stronger than when we embrace weakness, never more whole than when we're broken in His hands.

CHAPTER 12

UNION AND HOLINESS—LIVING FROM SANCTIFICATION, NOT FOR IT

THE FRUIT OF IDENTITY, NOT THE REQUIREMENT FOR ACCEPTANCE

Holiness is not a ladder we climb to reach God—it is the natural outworking of the God who already dwells within us. For many, the word *holiness* carries burdensome connotations: rules, moral pressure, or religious rigidity. But in the context of union, holiness is not a demand but a result. It is not something we achieve to get closer to God—it is what manifests because we are already one with Him.

Paul declares that Christ Himself "became for us wisdom from God—and righteousness and sanctification and redemption" (1 Corinthians 1:30). Sanctification is not a process we engineer—it is a person we contain. The call to holiness, then, is a call to live from what is already true in our spirit.

Jerry Bridges observed: "Holiness is not a series of do's and don'ts but a conformity to the character of God and obedience to the will of God."[139] This conformity flows from union, not toward it.

I. THE GIFT OF SANCTIFICATION

The New Testament affirms that every believer is already sanctified in Christ. Paul begins his letter to the Corinthians by addressing them as "those who are sanctified in Christ Jesus, called to be saints" (1 Corinthians 1:2). He does not speak of them as sinners trying to become holy, but as holy people learning to live like it.

Hebrews 10:10 confirms this: "We have been sanctified through the offering of the body of Jesus Christ once for all." This is positional sanctification—a completed act rooted in union. It is not based on behavior, but on blood. Our spirit has been made holy by Christ's indwelling presence (2 Corinthians 5:21).

Greek scholar Kenneth Wuest explains: "The Greek perfect tense used here indicates a past completed action with continuing results. We have been sanctified and remain in that state."[140]

This does not mean that holiness has no process—but it means the process starts from a finished place. The believer is not climbing toward holiness; they are learning to walk in what they already are.

II. HOLINESS AS IDENTITY, NOT ANXIETY

When sanctification is disconnected from union, it becomes anxiety. Believers begin striving to be holy enough, pure enough, righteous enough to be accepted or effective. But in Christ, we start from acceptance. "You are complete in Him" (Colossians 2:10). You are "a chosen generation, a royal priesthood, a holy nation" (1 Peter 2:9).

This identity-based holiness produces joy, not fear. It motivates purity not to avoid punishment but to express love. Jesus said, "If you love Me, keep My commandments" (John 14:15). Holiness is not a test of worth—it is a display of devotion.

J.I. Packer wrote: "Holiness is not primarily a matter of doing but of being. It is a matter of relationship with God through Jesus Christ."[141]

When the believer knows that Christ lives within, sin becomes unthinkable not because of fear of judgment, but because it contradicts the indwelling nature of their true identity. "How shall we who died to sin live any longer in it?" (Romans 6:2). We resist sin because we are new, not to become new.

III. THE PROCESS OF SANCTIFICATION: SOUL ALIGNING WITH SPIRIT

While the spirit is instantly made holy at salvation, the soul—the mind, will, and emotions—must be renewed. This is the process of progressive sanctification. Paul writes, "Be transformed by the renewing of your mind" (Romans 12:2). The mind must align with what is already true in the spirit.

This process is not about working harder—it is about beholding Jesus. "We all... beholding... are being transformed into the same image from glory to glory" (2 Corinthians 3:18). Transformation flows from vision, not performance.

Contemporary author John Ortberg explains: "Spiritual transformation is not a matter of trying harder, but of training wisely."[142] This training involves positioning ourselves to behold Christ and allowing His life to flow through us.

As we yield to the Spirit and abide in Christ, our attitudes, appetites, and actions begin to reflect His nature. Paul instructs, "Put on the new man who is renewed in knowledge according to the image of Him who created him" (Colossians 3:10). The new man is not fabricated—it is revealed.

IV. HOLINESS IS FREEDOM, NOT LEGALISM

Legalism makes holiness a condition for acceptance; union makes it the fruit of relationship. Legalism says, "Be holy so God will dwell with you." Union says, "God dwells in you, therefore live holy."

Paul confronted legalism repeatedly. To the Galatians, he warned, "Are you so foolish? Having begun in the Spirit, are you now being made perfect by the flesh?" (Galatians 3:3). They had received the Spirit through faith but were now returning to performance.

Philip Yancey distinguishes: "Legalism is looking to something besides Jesus Christ for salvation. Grace is looking to nothing but Jesus Christ."[143]

Jesus rebuked the Pharisees for their external holiness disconnected from inner transformation (Matthew 23:25-28). True holiness is not behavior modification—it is Christ-manifestation. It flows from the inside out.

Peter affirms this: "Be holy, for I am holy" (1 Peter 1:16). This is not a threat but a promise. Holiness is the natural result of having the Holy One dwelling within.

V. GRACE THAT TRAINS, NOT EXCUSES

Union-based holiness does not promote passivity. Grace is not permission to sin—it is power to live free from it. "For the grace of God... teaches us that, denying ungodliness and worldly lusts, we should live soberly, righteously, and godly" (Titus 2:11-12). Grace is a teacher, not just a covering.

Paul asks, "Shall we continue in sin that grace may abound? Certainly not! How shall we who died to sin live any longer in it?" (Romans 6:1-2). Grace trains us to walk in victory, not to tolerate compromise.

Dallas Willard emphasized: "Grace is not opposed to effort, it is opposed to earning. Earning is an attitude. Effort is an action. Grace, you know, does not just have to do with forgiveness of sins alone."[144]

Holiness does not restrict life—it protects it. It is not the end of joy, but its source. "In Your presence is fullness of joy" (Psalm 16:11). Holiness makes room for deeper union, clearer hearing, and unbroken fellowship.

VI. HOLINESS AS WITNESS

The world is watching for authenticity. Holiness is not about being religious—it is about being real. When believers live in purity, peace, integrity, and love, they manifest Christ. "Let your light so shine before men, that they may see your good works and glorify your Father in heaven" (Matthew 5:16).

Holiness is evangelistic. It draws others not through perfection but through presence—the unmistakable presence of Christ seen in a set-apart life. Paul exhorts, "Walk in wisdom toward outsiders... Let your speech always be gracious" (Colossians 4:5-6).

Charles Spurgeon noted: "A holy life will produce the deepest impression. Lighthouses blow no horns; they only shine."[145]

In a culture that mocks purity, downplays sin, and celebrates indulgence, a holy life is prophetic. It declares that Christ is real, union is possible, and joy is found in obedience.

VII. CORPORATE HOLINESS

Holiness is not just individual; it's corporate. The church is called to be "a holy nation" (1 Peter 2:9). This corporate holiness creates a culture where:

1. **Truth is spoken in love** (Ephesians 4:15)

2. **Sin is addressed redemptively** (Galatians 6:1)

3. **Purity is celebrated, not mocked** (Philippians 4:8)

4. **Weakness is supported, not exploited** (1 Thessalonians 5:14)

5. **Christ's character is collectively displayed** (Ephesians 4:1-3)

When churches prioritize being "seeker-friendly" over being holy, they lose their prophetic edge. But when they embrace corporate holiness, they become cities on a hill.

VIII. HOLINESS IN DAILY LIFE

Practical holiness touches every area of life:

1. **Thoughts**: "Whatever things are true...noble...just...pure...lovely...think on these things" (Philippians 4:8).

2. **Speech**: "Let no corrupt word proceed out of your mouth" (Ephesians 4:29).

3. **Relationships**: "Be kind to one another, tenderhearted, forgiving" (Ephesians 4:32).

4. **Work**: "Whatever you do, do it heartily, as to the Lord" (Colossians 3:23).

5. **Money**: "You cannot serve God and mammon" (Matthew 6:24).

6. **Sexuality**: "Flee sexual immorality" (1 Corinthians 6:18).

7. **Entertainment**: "I will set nothing wicked before my eyes" (Psalm 101:3).

Holiness isn't about withdrawal from the world but engagement with it from a different source—the indwelling Christ.

IX. THE JOY OF HOLINESS

Contrary to popular belief, holiness produces joy, not misery. The holy life is the happy life because it aligns with our true design. Sin promises freedom but delivers bondage; holiness seems restrictive but brings liberty.

C.S. Lewis observed: "How little people know who think that holiness is dull. When one meets the real thing...it is irresistible."[146]

The Psalms repeatedly connect holiness with joy:

- "In Your presence is fullness of joy" (Psalm 16:11)

- "The joy of the LORD is your strength" (Nehemiah 8:10)

- "Happy are the people whose God is the LORD!" (Psalm 144:15)

When holiness flows from union rather than duty, it becomes delightful rather than drudgery.

X. GROWING IN HOLINESS

While holiness is rooted in our position in Christ, we can cooperate with the Spirit's work through:

1. **Beholding Christ**: We become like what we behold (2 Corinthians 3:18).

2. **Renewing the Mind**: Replacing lies with truth (Romans 12:2).

3. **Practicing Presence**: Living aware of Christ within (Colossians 1:27).

4. **Confession and Repentance**: Keeping short accounts with God (1 John 1:9).

5. **Community Accountability**: Iron sharpening iron (Proverbs 27:17).

6. **Spiritual Disciplines**: Training, not trying (1 Timothy 4:7).

7. **Yielding to the Spirit**: Letting Him produce His fruit (Galatians 5:22-23).

Remember, growing in holiness isn't about becoming more acceptable to God—it's about expressing more fully the holy nature He's already placed within us.

As we live from our union with Christ, holiness becomes not a burden to bear but a beauty to behold—the natural expression of Christ's life flowing through us. This is the holiness that attracts rather than repels, that invites rather than intimidates, that demonstrates the reality of our union with the Holy One.

THE ULTIMATE UNION—GLORY REVEALED

FROM PRESENT COMMUNION TO FUTURE CONFORMATION

Union with Christ is not just the beginning of the Christian life—it is its destination. What began as a spiritual reality in the secret place of the soul will one day be revealed openly and gloriously. The union that is now known by faith will one day be seen by sight. The One who now indwells us invisibly will one day appear in glory—and in that moment, we will discover that His glory is not separate from us, but shared with us.

The apostle John declared this with wonder: "Beloved, now we are children of God; and it has not yet been revealed what we shall be, but we know that when He is revealed, we shall be like Him, for we shall see Him as He is" (1 John 3:2). The full manifestation of our union with Christ will be unveiled at His appearing. Until then, we live between the already and the not yet—fully united, but not yet fully glorified.

I. OUR GLORIFICATION IS THE UNVEILING OF OUR UNION

Paul affirms this future hope in Romans 8:17: "If indeed we suffer with Him, that we may also be glorified together." Glorification is not a separate reward—it is the culmination of union. To be glorified with Christ is to be conformed fully to His image, spirit, soul, and body. "Whom He justified, these He also glorified" (Romans 8:30).

105

Anthony Hoekema explains: "Glorification is the final step in the application of redemption. It will happen when Christ returns and raises the dead. Then believers will be completely and permanently delivered from all sin and its results."[147]

This glory is not human applause or religious fame—it is the radiant manifestation of Christ's indwelling life. "When Christ who is our life appears, then you also will appear with Him in glory" (Colossians 3:4). His return will not just reveal Him—it will reveal us. Not because we have become divine, but because divine life has become visible in us.

Until then, "we groan within ourselves, eagerly waiting for the adoption, the redemption of our body" (Romans 8:23). Our spirit is already one with Christ. Our soul is being renewed. But our bodies still await transformation. Glorification completes the circle of union: spirit, soul, and body fully filled and formed by Christ.

II. THE MARRIAGE SUPPER: UNION IN FULL CELEBRATION

The culmination of our union is portrayed in Revelation 19 as a wedding: "The marriage of the Lamb has come, and His wife has made herself ready" (Revelation 19:7). This is not just poetic imagery—it is prophetic fulfillment. Our union with Christ, now spiritual, will be eternally celebrated in shared glory.

Jesus spoke of this when He promised, "I go to prepare a place for you... that where I am, there you may be also" (John 14:2-3). His goal is not distance but dwelling. The church is not just an army or a temple—it is a bride. And the bride is not meant for mere service, but for shared life.

G.K. Beale notes: "The marriage metaphor emphasizes the intimate, permanent, and exclusive nature of the relationship between Christ and His people. It's the consummation of the union that began at conversion."[148]

Paul understood this mystery when he wrote, "This is a great mystery, but I speak concerning Christ and the church" (Ephesians 5:32). The eternal destiny of the redeemed is not simply to be near Christ, but to be one with Him forever, in joy, rest, worship, and partnership in the age to come.

III. PRESENT HOPE THAT PURIFIES

While the glory of our future union is unspeakably great, it is not disconnected from the present. John writes, "Everyone who has this hope in Him purifies himself, just as He is pure" (1 John 3:3). The vision of future glory motivates present holiness. It anchors our hearts amid trials, and it calls us to live with eternal focus.

Paul exhorts, "If then you were raised with Christ, seek those things which are above... Set your mind on things above, not on things on the earth" (Colossians 3:1-2). The believer who lives with eternity in view walks differently—not because of fear, but because of love. We live not to earn glory, but because we have been united to the Glorious One.

N.T. Wright observes: "The Christian hope is not about 'going to heaven when you die' but about God's new creation, the joining of heaven and earth, and our participation in that through resurrection."[149]

Even now, we are "being transformed... from glory to glory" (2 Corinthians 3:18). Our present transformation is a preview of our coming glorification. Each moment of surrender, each step of obedience, each gaze of worship is shaping us for that final unveiling.

IV. UNION IS THE ETERNAL REALITY

When all ministry ends, union will remain. When assignments shift, union endures. When prophecy ceases and knowledge passes away, "we shall know just as we also are known" (1 Corinthians 13:12). The heart of salvation is not activity—it is union. The reward of the believer is not a mansion—it is the Man Christ Jesus.

This is why Paul said, "To live is Christ, and to die is gain" (Philippians 1:21). Death is not the loss of purpose—it is the entrance into perfect union. No more distortion, distraction, or distance. Just unbroken, unveiled, face-to-face life with the One who has already made us one with Himself.

Richard Baxter wrote: "The saints' everlasting rest is the most blessed state of a Christian having obtained the end of his faith, even the salvation of his soul, by the full enjoyment of God to all eternity."[150]

The vision of the New Jerusalem captures this beautifully: "Behold, the tabernacle of God is with men, and He will dwell with them, and they shall be His people" (Revelation 21:3). Union is not just a New Testament theme—it is the eternal reality for which all creation groans.

V. THE ALREADY AND THE NOT YET

We live in the tension between what is already true and what is not yet visible:

Already	Not Yet
United with Christ	Fully glorified
Seated in heavenly places	Physically transformed
Complete in Him	Completely conformed
Hidden with Christ in God	Revealed with Christ in glory
Children of God	Fully manifested as sons

This tension creates both hope and humility. Hope because our future is secure; humility because our present experience is partial.

VI. CREATION'S PARTICIPATION

Our glorification affects all creation. Paul writes, "The creation eagerly waits for the revealing of the sons of God... because the creation itself also will be delivered from the bondage of corruption into the glorious liberty of the children of God" (Romans 8:19, 21).

Our union with Christ has cosmic implications. As we are fully revealed as God's children, creation itself will be renewed. The new heavens and new earth are not separate from our glorification but intimately connected to it.

VII. THE BEATIFIC VISION

The church fathers spoke of the "beatific vision"—the direct sight of God that brings perfect happiness. Thomas Aquinas taught that this vision is the essence of eternal life.[151]

But through union with Christ, we understand this vision differently. It's not merely seeing God from outside but seeing

Him from within—through our eternal union with Christ. We will know as we are known, love as we are loved, and live as we are lived in.

Jonathan Edwards described it: "The enjoyment of God is the only happiness with which our souls can be satisfied... Fathers and mothers, husbands, wives, or children, or the company of earthly friends, are but shadows; but God is the substance."[152]

VIII. IMPLICATIONS FOR PRESENT LIVING

Understanding our ultimate union shapes how we live now:

1. Eternal Perspective: "Our light affliction, which is but for a moment, is working for us a far more exceeding and eternal weight of glory" (2 Corinthians 4:17).

2. Present Contentment: Knowing our future glory helps us hold earthly things loosely.

3. Bold Witness: The certainty of glory emboldens us to share Christ fearlessly.

4. Patient Endurance: "If we endure, we shall also reign with Him" (2 Timothy 2:12).

5. Joyful Anticipation: "Looking for the blessed hope and glorious appearing of our great God and Savior Jesus Christ" (Titus 2:13).

IX. THE FINAL PRAYER

Jesus' prayer in John 17 will be fully answered: "That they all may be one, as You, Father, are in Me, and I in You; that they also may be one in Us... that they may be one just as We are one: I in them, and You in Me; that they may be made perfect in one" (John 17:21-23).

This perfect unity—with God and with each other—is the ultimate destiny of all who are in Christ. It's not uniformity but perfect harmony, not absorption but perfect communion.

X. CLOSING EXHORTATION: ABIDE UNTIL GLORY APPEARS

Until that day, the invitation remains: "Abide in Me, and I in you" (John 15:4). Abide when it's easy, abide when it's costly. Abide when the crowds cheer, and when no one sees. Abide when you understand, and when mystery surrounds you. Your life is not your own—it is hidden with Christ in God.

Let your ministry flow from this place. Let your joy be anchored in this place. Let your identity, your holiness, your peace, your perseverance, and your purpose all flow from this one reality: You are one spirit with the Lord (1 Corinthians 6:17).

And when He appears, you will appear with Him in glory—not as a stranger looking from afar, but as one who has already been joined in secret and now shines in full.

Teresa of Avila captured this hope beautifully: "Christ has no body now but yours, No hands, no feet on earth but yours. Yours are the eyes through which He looks With compassion on this world. Yours are the feet with which He walks to do good. Yours are the hands with which He blesses all the world."[153]

Perfect Union

This is our present calling and our eternal destiny—to be so united with Christ that His life flows through us now and His glory shines in us forever. May we live each day in the light of this glorious union, until faith becomes sight and we see Him face to face.

FREQUENTLY ASKED QUESTIONS ABOUT UNION WITH CHRIST

Clarifying What It Means to Live from Our Oneness with Him

Union with Christ is a transformative and liberating truth, yet it can raise sincere questions—especially for those coming out of performance-based religious systems or who are just beginning to grasp the reality of indwelling life. Below are some frequently asked questions, with biblical and theological responses to help clarify this vital doctrine.

Is union with Christ the same as losing my individuality?

No. Union with Christ does not erase your uniqueness—it fulfills it. Just as Jesus remained fully Himself while being one with the Father (John 10:30; 17:21), so too the believer remains a distinct person while being united with Christ. God did not come to destroy human personhood but to redeem and indwell it.

C.S. Lewis explained: "The more we get what we now call 'ourselves' out of the way and let Him take us over, the more truly ourselves we become... It is when I turn to Christ, when I give myself up to His personality, that I first begin to have a real personality of my own."[154]

Union with Christ means that your true identity is now defined by His indwelling life. Your gifts, personality, and calling (assignment) are now animated by His Spirit, not your flesh.

Paul affirms this when he says, "I no longer live, but Christ lives in me" (Galatians 2:20). You are still "you," but now you are the "you" God intended from the beginning—alive in Christ.

If I am already holy in Christ, why do I still struggle with sin?

Because while your **spirit** has been made new and holy through union (1 Corinthians 6:17; Hebrews 10:10), your **soul and body** are still being renewed (Romans 12:2; 1 Thessalonians 5:23). This is the process of progressive sanctification—learning to manifest outwardly what is already true inwardly.

Sin struggles do not negate union. In fact, they are often the very areas where union must be believed more deeply. The goal is not to earn victory but to enforce it—by walking in the Spirit, renewing the mind, and depending daily on the indwelling life of Christ. "Sin shall not have dominion over you, for you are not under law but under grace" (Romans 6:14).

Martin Luther described this tension as being "simultaneously justified and sinner" (simul justus et peccator).[155] We are fully righteous in our position but still battling sin in our practice.

How does union with Christ relate to grace?

Union is the **goal and vehicle** of grace. Grace is not just unmerited favor—it is the divine influence that enables us to partake in the life of God (2 Peter 1:4). Through grace, we are not merely forgiven—we are joined to Jesus Himself. Grace is both the invitation and the empowerment to live in union.

Paul writes that "of His fullness we have all received, and grace upon grace" (John 1:16). That fullness is Christ. Grace brings us into union and keeps us abiding there. It is not an excuse to sin but the power to live holy—because Christ, who is our holiness, lives within.

If I'm already united with Christ, do I still need spiritual disciplines?

Yes—but their purpose changes. Spiritual disciplines (prayer, Scripture, worship, fasting) are no longer methods to *achieve* God's presence or favor. They are means of awareness—ways of attuning our hearts to the indwelling Christ and allowing His life to flow more freely.

Richard Foster clarifies: "The disciplines are God's way of getting us into the ground; they put us where He can work within us and transform us."[156]

Paul says, "Exercise yourself toward godliness" (1 Timothy 4:7). Disciplines are not self-improvement strategies. They are responses to divine indwelling. When practiced from union, spiritual disciplines become life-giving and joyful, not legalistic or burdensome. "Abide in Me, and I in you... apart from Me you can do nothing" (John 15:4-5).

What if I don't always feel close to God?

Feelings are not the foundation of union—faith is. Christ lives in you whether or not you feel Him in a given moment (2 Corinthians 13:5). Union is not a mood; it is a covenantal reality. "We walk by faith, not by sight" (2 Corinthians 5:7).

When emotions fluctuate, return to what the Word declares: "I will never leave you nor forsake you" (Hebrews 13:5). Feelings may serve as indicators, but they are not final authorities. Renew your mind with the truth of union, and feelings will often follow.

Can union with Christ be lost?

Union is established by grace through faith (Ephesians 2:8) and sealed by the indwelling of the Holy Spirit (Ephesians 1:13). It is a covenant, not a contract. However, Scripture—**Prayer as Presence**—Prayer is not simply petitions but positioning. "I have set the Lord always before me" (Psalm 16:8). To behold in prayer is to speak and listen with full awareness that Christ is in us.

- **Scripture as Revelation** – The entire Bible points to Christ (Luke 24:27). Studying Scripture as a lens to behold Him—rather than simply mining for principles—transforms the mind and spirit.

UNION WITH CHRIST IN HISTORICAL CHRISTIAN THOUGHT

A STREAM OF REVELATION ACROSS THE AGES

While modern Christianity often emphasizes individual salvation or external forms of spirituality, the reality of union with Christ has remained a hidden thread, woven throughout the history of the believing community. From the apostles onward, men and women filled with the Spirit recognized that the center of the faith was not merely believing certain facts or performing certain duties—it was living in vital, experiential communion with Christ Himself.

The language, emphasis, and theological expressions varied, but the heartbeat remained: believers are called not merely to follow Christ from a distance, but to participate in His very life. This appendix explores key movements and voices that, across the centuries, kept this truth alive.

1. The Apostolic Witness: Union as the Foundation

The apostles were the first to articulate union clearly. Paul spoke constantly of being "in Christ" (over 160 times in his letters). John wrote of abiding in Christ and Christ abiding in us (John 15:4-5; 1 John 4:13). Peter declared that believers are "partakers of the divine nature" (2 Peter 1:4).

Union was not a mystical idea reserved for the few—it was presented as the normal Christian life. It framed their understanding of salvation, sanctification, and glorification. To be saved was to be placed into Christ; to grow was to abide more deeply in Christ; to hope was to anticipate the full unveiling of life with Christ.

James D.G. Dunn notes: "Paul's 'in Christ' language is not metaphorical but describes the most fundamental reality of Christian existence."[158]

2. Early Communities: Communion Over Institution

In the generations immediately following the apostles, union remained a central theme—especially among persecuted believers who had no institutional power. These early communities emphasized intimate fellowship with God through Christ, often meeting in homes, caves, or secret gatherings.

Their understanding of union was practical and relational. To be baptized was seen as being grafted into Christ's death and resurrection (Romans 6:3-5). Communion (the Lord's Supper) was celebrated not as mere ritual but as real participation in the life of Christ (1 Corinthians 10:16).

The Didache (c. 100 AD) instructs: "Let no one eat or drink of your Eucharist except those who have been baptized into the name of the Lord; for concerning this also the Lord has said, 'Give not that which is holy to the dogs.'"[159] This reflects their view of communion as sacred participation in Christ.

The focus was not building religious systems but living from an indwelling Christ, even in the face of suffering and martyrdom.

3. The Eastern Witness: Participation in Divine Life

Among Eastern believers, especially those writing in the Syriac and Greek-speaking regions, the doctrine of *participation* (*koinonia* or *theosis*) became a central way of describing salvation.

The term theosis—meaning becoming partakers of divine nature—was based squarely on 2 Peter 1:4. This teaching did not mean absorption into God's essence (as in pantheism), but sharing by grace in His life, love, and holiness.

Writers like Ephrem the Syrian and later Eastern voices emphasized that salvation was more than judicial pardon—it was healing, restoration, and communion. They often spoke of Christ's incarnation as God "taking on our humanity so we could partake of His divinity."

Athanasius famously declared: "The Word became human so that humans might participate in the divine nature."[160] This wasn't suggesting we become divine in essence, but that we participate in divine life through union with Christ.

This emphasis preserved the mystery and intimacy of union without dissolving the distinction between Creator and creature.

4. The Reformers: Rediscovering Union Through Justification

During the Reformation (16th century), when corruption and legalism had heavily distorted the church, God raised up reformers to re-center the faith on grace and Christ alone.

While figures like Martin Luther and John Clayton are often associated with *justification by faith,* a deeper reading of their works shows that **union with Christ** undergirded even their teaching on justification.

- Luther spoke of the "joyful exchange": our sin is placed on Christ and His righteousness placed on us—not by merit, but by mystical union through faith. He wrote: "Faith unites the soul with Christ as a bride is united with her bridegroom."[161]

- Clayton called union with Christ the "sum of all blessings" and insisted that all benefits of salvation (justification, sanctification, adoption) flow from being united to Him. He wrote: "First, we must understand that as long as Christ remains outside of us, and we are separated from him, all that he has suffered and done for the salvation of the human race remains useless and of no value for us."[162]

Thus, the Reformation's battle cry was not merely against works-righteousness; it was a call back to abiding in Christ alone.

5. The Puritans: Union as Experiential Reality

The Puritans took the Reformation insights and emphasized their experiential dimension. They wrote extensively about communion with God, the indwelling Christ, and the believer's mystical union with Him.

John Owen wrote a masterpiece titled "Communion with God," where he explored how believers fellowship with each person of the Godhead. About union with Christ, he wrote: "The greatest sorrow and burden you can lay upon the Father, the greatest unkindness you can do to him, is not to believe that he loves you."[163]

Thomas Goodwin emphasized: "Christ is yours and you are His—there is nothing that Christ has that is not yours."[164]

Richard Sibbes taught: "We are mystically united to Christ by faith... There is a blessed union between Christ and us, whence flows all good things."[165]

6. Mystics and Devotional Writers: Abiding as Daily Life

Throughout history, a stream of believers—sometimes called mystics or devotional writers—sought to live in conscious, daily communion with Christ.

Figures like Brother Lawrence *(The Practice of the Presence of God)* and Madame Guyon *(Experiencing the Depths of Jesus Christ)* described union as not an abstract idea but an immediate experience of walking with the indwelling Christ moment by moment.

Brother Lawrence famously said, "The time of business does not with me differ from the time of prayer."[166] For him, washing dishes was as holy as praying in the chapel if done with awareness of God's presence.

Teresa of Avila described stages of prayer that led to "spiritual marriage" with Christ—the highest form of union available in this life.[167]

Though sometimes misunderstood or marginalized by institutional structures, these voices kept alive the truth that union was meant to saturate everyday life—not just church life.

7. The Holiness Movement: Union as the Source of Sanctification

In the 18th and 19th centuries, the Holiness movement arose, emphasizing the believer's call to holy living. While some streams became legalistic, the best representatives understood that holiness flows from union with Christ.

John Wesley taught about Christian perfection, which he defined not as sinlessness but as being perfected in love through union with Christ. He wrote: "By justification we are saved from the guilt of sin, and restored to the favor of God; by sanctification we are saved from the power and root of sin, and restored to the image of God."[168]

Phoebe Palmer emphasized the "altar sanctifies the gift"— teaching that as believers place themselves fully on Christ (the altar), they are sanctified through union with Him.[169]

8. Modern Echoes: Recovering Union Today

In recent centuries, various renewal movements have re-emphasized life in the Spirit and union with Christ. Pentecostal and charismatic believers, while focusing on the empowerment of the Spirit, have in many streams returned to the truth that the Christian life is about carrying the presence of God, not merely performing religious duties.

Scholars like Michael Gorman, N.T. Wright, and Constantine Campbell have called modern theology back to seeing salvation not merely as transactional but participatory—rooted in union with the crucified and risen Messiah.

Rankin Wilbourne's "Union with Christ" and Marcus Peter Johnson's "One with Christ" represent contemporary efforts to recover this central biblical theme for today's church.[170]

Today, amidst both religious formalism and cultural secularism, the Spirit is once again awakening the people of God to the centrality of union: Christ in you, the hope of glory (Colossians 1:27).

9. Common Threads Through History

Despite different eras, cultures, and theological emphases, several themes consistently appear in discussions of union with Christ:

1. **Identity Over Activity**: Being precedes doing.

2. **Presence Over Performance**: God's indwelling matters more than our efforts.

3. **Participation Not Imitation**: We share Christ's life, not just copy His example.

4. **Rest Not Striving**: Spiritual life flows from abiding, not achieving.

5. **Corporate Expression**: Union with Christ means union with His body.

6. **Already But Not Yet**: Present union awaits future glorification.

7. **Cross and Resurrection**: Union is grounded in Christ's death and life.

CLOSING REFLECTION: AN ANCIENT, LIVING REALITY

Union with Christ is not a new doctrine—it is the ancient heartbeat of the faith. It has survived persecution, distortion, neglect, and revival. It is not the invention of theologians—it is the gift of God, revealed in His Word, embodied by Christ, and made alive by the Spirit.

From the underground house churches of the first century to persecuted believers today, the testimony remains the same: **"I have been crucified with Christ; it is no longer I who live, but Christ lives in me" (Galatians 2:20).**

Union is the treasure of the redeemed—and its full glory is yet to be revealed.

ENDNOTES

[1] James D.G. Dunn, *The Theology of Paul the Apostle* (Grand Rapids: Eerdmans, 1998), 390-401.

[2] E.P. Sanders, *Paul and Palestinian Judaism* (Minneapolis: Fortress Press, 1977), 456-463.

[3] Raymond E. Brown, *The Gospel According to John* (New York: Doubleday, 1970), 86-92.

[4] Mark S. Smith, *The Origins of Biblical Monotheism: Israel's Polytheistic Background and the Ugaritic Texts* (New York: Oxford University Press, 2001), 143-148.

[5] D.A. Carson, *The Gospel According to John* (Grand Rapids: Eerdmans, 1991), 394-395.

[6] Larry W. Hurtado, *One God, One Lord: Early Christian Devotion and Ancient Jewish Monotheism* (Philadelphia: Fortress Press, 1988), 93-124.

[7] Jacob Neusner, *The Mishnah: A New Translation* (New Haven: Yale University Press, 1988), 645-647.

[8] Joachim Jeremias, *The Prayers of Jesus* (London: SCM Press, 1967), 57-65.

[9] Joel Marcus, *Mark 8-16: A New Translation with Introduction and Commentary* (New Haven: Yale University Press, 2009), 982-988.

[10] Ben Witherington III, *The Christology of Jesus* (Minneapolis: Fortress Press, 1990), 184-187.

[11] Craig S. Keener, *The Gospel of John: A Commentary* (Peabody: Hendrickson, 2003), 679-684.

[12] Richard Bauckham, *God Crucified: Monotheism and Christology in the New Testament* (Grand Rapids: Eerdmans, 1999), 67-73.

[13] Gerald F. Hawthorne, *The Presence and the Power: The Significance of the Holy Spirit in the Life and Ministry of Jesus* (Dallas: Word Publishing, 1991), 208-215.

[14] Max Turner, *Power from on High: The Spirit in Israel's Restoration and Witness in Luke-Acts* (Sheffield: Sheffield Academic Press, 1996), 346-351.

[15] Andrew T. Lincoln, *The Gospel According to St. John* (London: Continuum, 2005), 430-435.

[16] John H. Walton, *Genesis 1 as Ancient Cosmology* (Winona Lake: Eisenbrauns, 2011), 172-178.

[17] Marc Cortez, *Theological Anthropology: A Guide for the Perplexed* (London: T&T Clark, 2010), 42-48.

[18] Frank Moore Cross, *From Epic to Canon: History and Literature in Ancient Israel* (Baltimore: Johns Hopkins University Press, 1998), 13-22.

[19] Terence E. Fretheim, *Exodus* (Louisville: John Knox Press, 1991), 269-274.

[20] John Goldingay, *Isaiah* (Grand Rapids: Baker Academic, 2001), 235-241.

²¹ Craig R. Koester, *Symbolism in the Fourth Gospel: Meaning, Mystery, Community* (Minneapolis: Fortress Press, 2003), 128-135.

²² James D.G. Dunn, *"The Theology of Paul the Apostle,"* in *The Cambridge Companion to St. Paul,* ed. *James D.G. Dunn* (Cambridge: Cambridge University Press, 2003), 91-104.

²³ Constantine R. Campbell, *Paul and Union with Christ: An Exegetical and Theological Study* (Grand Rapids: Zondervan, 2012), 413-421.

²⁴ Raymond E. Brown, *The Community of the Beloved Disciple* (New York: Paulist Press, 1979), 189-196.

²⁵ Richard Bauckham, *Jude, 2 Peter, Word Biblical Commentary* (Waco: Word Books, 1983), 181-188.

²⁶ G.K. Beale, *The Temple and the Church's Mission: A Biblical Theology of the Dwelling Place of God* (Downers Grove: InterVarsity Press, 2004), 313-318.

²⁷ Michael Horton, *Covenant and Salvation: Union with Christ* (Louisville: Westminster John Knox Press, 2007), 267-271.

²⁸ Douglas J. Moo, *The Epistle to the Romans, New International Commentary on the New Testament* (Grand Rapids: Eerdmans, 1996), 328-334.

²⁹ Murray J. Harris, *The Second Epistle to the Corinthians, New International Greek Testament Commentary* (Grand Rapids: Eerdmans, 2005), 432-438.

³⁰ Gordon D. Fee, *The First Epistle to the Corinthians, New International Commentary on the New Testament* (Grand Rapids: Eerdmans, 1987), 31-36.

[31] Herman N. Ridderbos, *Paul: An Outline of His Theology*, trans. *John Richard de Witt* (Grand Rapids: Eerdmans, 1975), 253-258.

[32] F.F. Bruce, *The Epistle to the Galatians, New International Greek Testament Commentary* (Grand Rapids: Eerdmans, 1982), 144-149.

[33] Richard N. Longenecker, *Galatians, Word Biblical Commentary* (Dallas: Word Books, 1990), 154-159.

[34] James M. Scott, *Adoption as Sons of God: An Exegetical Investigation into the Background of* ΥΙΟΘΕΣΙΑ *in the Pauline Corpus* (Tübingen: Mohr Siebeck, 1992), 267-272.

[35] Peter H. Davids, *The Letters of 2 Peter and Jude, Pillar New Testament Commentary* (Grand Rapids: Eerdmans, 2006), 175-180.

[36] Oscar Cullmann, *Christ and Time: The Primitive Christian Conception of Time and History*, trans. Floyd V. Filson (Philadelphia: Westminster Press, 1950), 81-88.

[37] Michael J. Gorman, *Cruciformity: Paul's Narrative Spirituality of the Cross* (Grand Rapids: Eerdmans, 2001), 357-362.

[38] Michael J. Gorman, *Inhabiting the Cruciform God: Kenosis, Justification, and Theosis in Paul's Narrative Soteriology* (Grand Rapids: Eerdmans, 2009), 161-167.

[39] Markus Barth, *Ephesians: Introduction, Translation, and Commentary on Chapters 1-3, Anchor Bible* (Garden City: Doubleday, 1974), 309-315.

[40] James D.G. Dunn, "*Paul's Understanding of the Death of*

Jesus as Sacrifice, " in *Sacrifice and Redemption: Durham Essays in Theology*, ed. S.W. Sykes (Cambridge: Cambridge University Press, 1991), 35-49.

[41] Michael J. Gorman, *Reading Paul* (Eugene: Cascade Books, 2008), 57-63.

[42] N.T. Wright, *Paul and the Faithfulness of God* (Minneapolis: Fortress Press, 2013), 634-641.

[43] Robert Letham, *Union with Christ: In Scripture, History, and Theology* (Phillipsburg: P&R Publishing, 2011), 1-8.

[44] Daniel B. Wallace, *Greek Grammar Beyond the Basics* (Grand Rapids: Zondervan, 1996), 554-565.

[45] John Murray, *Redemption Accomplished and Applied* (Grand Rapids: Eerdmans, 1955), 161-168.

[46] F.F. Bruce, *Paul: Apostle of the Heart Set Free* (Grand Rapids: Eerdmans, 1977), 199-206.

[47] Augustine of Hippo, *Sermons on Selected Lessons of the New Testament*, trans. R.G. MacMullen, in Nicene and Post-Nicene Fathers, First Series, vol. 6, ed. Philip Schaff (Buffalo: Christian Literature Company, 1888), 252-258.

[48] Sinclair B. Ferguson, *The Christian Life: A Doctrinal Introduction* (London: Hodder & Stoughton, 1989), 81-87.

[49] D.A. Carson, *The Gospel According to John* (Grand Rapids: Eerdmans, 1991), 520-527.

[50] Francis Brown, S.R. Driver, and Charles A. Briggs, *The Brown-Driver-Briggs Hebrew and English Lexicon* (Peabody: Hendrickson, 1996), 701-702.

[51] Dallas Willard, *The Divine Conspiracy: Rediscovering Our Hidden Life in God* (San Francisco: HarperSanFrancisco, 1998), 338-342.

[52] J.I. Packer, *Knowing God* (Downers Grove: InterVarsity Press, 1993), 206-213.

[53] Timothy Keller, *The Prodigal God: Recovering the Heart of the Christian Faith* (New York: Dutton, 2008), 19-26.

[54] Joachim Jeremias, *The Prayers of Jesus, Studies in Biblical Theology* (London: SCM Press, 1967), 57-65.

[55] Klyne Snodgrass, *Ephesians,* NIV Application Commentary (Grand Rapids: Zondervan, 1996), 200-207.

[56] Dietrich Bonhoeffer, *Life Together,* trans. John W. Doberstein (New York: Harper & Row, 1954), 35-41.

[57] Rankin Wilbourne, *Union with Christ: The Way to Know and Enjoy God* (Colorado Springs: David C. Cook, 2016), 45-52.

[58] John Calvin, *Institutes of the Christian Religion,* ed. John T. McNeill, trans. Ford Lewis Battles, Library of Christian Classics (Philadelphia: Westminster Press, 1960), 3.1.1.

[59] John Owen, *Communion with God,* ed. R.J.K. Law (Edinburgh: Banner of Truth, 1991), 9-16.

[60] Bernard of Clairvaux, *Selected Works,* trans. G.R. Evans (Mahwah: Paulist Press, 1987), 216-224.

[61] Neil T. Anderson, *Victory over the Darkness: Realizing the Power of Your Identity in Christ* (Ventura: Regal Books, 2000), 47-54.

[62] Abraham Joshua Heschel, *The Sabbath: Its Meaning for Modern Man* (New York: Farrar, Straus and Giroux, 1951), 14-21.

[63] James H. Charlesworth, ed., *The Old Testament Pseudepigrapha*, vol. 2 (Garden City: Doubleday, 1985), 55-63.

[64] Florentino García Martínez, *The Dead Sea Scrolls Translated: The Qumran Texts in English*, trans. Wilfred G.E. Watson (Leiden: Brill, 1994), 420-428.

[65] Frederick Dale Bruner, *Matthew: A Commentary*, vol. 1 (Grand Rapids: Eerdmans, 2004), 527-535.

[66] Michael Horton, *The Christian Faith: A Systematic Theology for Pilgrims on the Way* (Grand Rapids: Zondervan, 2011), 659-667.

[67] Douglas J. Moo, *Galatians, Baker Exegetical Commentary on the New Testament* (Grand Rapids: Baker Academic, 2013), 193-200.

[68] Ruth Haley Barton, *Sacred Rhythms: Arranging Our Lives for Spiritual Transformation* (Downers Grove: InterVarsity Press, 2006), 73-79.

[69] John Eldredge, *Walking with God: Talk to Him. Hear from Him. Really.* (Nashville: Thomas Nelson, 2008), 89-95.

[70] Evagrius Ponticus, *The Praktikos and Chapters on Prayer*, trans. John Eudes Bamberger (Kalamazoo: Cistercian Publications, 1981), 63-70.

[71] Meister Eckhart, *Selected Writings*, trans. Oliver Davies (London: Penguin, 1994), 178-184.

[72] Richard Sibbes, *The Complete Works of Richard Sibbes,* ed. Alexander B. Grosart (Edinburgh: James Nichol, 1862), 3:432-438.

[73] Jürgen Moltmann, *The Coming of God: Christian Eschatology,* trans. Margaret Kohl (Minneapolis: Fortress Press, 1996), 265-271.

[74] Watchman Nee, *The Normal Christian Life* (Wheaton: Tyndale House, 1977), 41-47.

[75] A.T. Robertson, *Word Pictures in the New Testament* (Nashville: Broadman Press, 1933), 5:324-325.

[76] Andrew Murray, *Abide in Christ* (London: Nisbet & Co., 1882), 28-35.

[77] Thomas F. Torrance, *The Mediation of Christ* (Grand Rapids: Eerdmans, 1983), 94-101.

[78] Herman Ridderbos, *The Coming of the Kingdom,* trans. H. de Jongste (Philadelphia: Presbyterian and Reformed Publishing Company, 1962), 303-310.

[79] Richard J. Foster, *Celebration of Discipline: The Path to Spiritual Growth* (San Francisco: Harper & Row, 1978), 6-12.

[80] Henri J.M. Nouwen, *The Way of the Heart: Desert Spirituality and Contemporary Ministry* (New York: Seabury Press, 1981), 15-21.

[81] Martin Luther, *Luther's Works,* ed. Jaroslav Pelikan (St. Louis: Concordia Publishing House, 1955), 31:12-18.

[82] Steven Barabas, *So Great Salvation: The History and Message of the Keswick Convention* (Eugene: Wipf & Stock, 2005), 51-57.

83 Howard Taylor, *Hudson Taylor's Spiritual Secret* (Chicago: Moody Publishers, 2009), 149-155.

84 Bill Johnson, *When Heaven Invades Earth: A Practical Guide to a Life of Miracles* (Shippensburg: Destiny Image, 2003), 87-93.

85 Dallas Willard, *Renovation of the Heart: Putting on the Character of Christ* (Colorado Springs: NavPress, 2002), 95-101.

86 Watchman Nee, *The Spiritual Man* (New York: Christian Fellowship Publishers, 1968), 1:31-37.

87 Caroline Leaf, *Switch On Your Brain: The Key to Peak Happiness, Thinking, and Health* (Grand Rapids: Baker Books, 2013), 33-40.

88 Scot McKnight, *The Blue Parakeet: Rethinking How You Read the Bible* (Grand Rapids: Zondervan, 2008), 67-73.

89 George Lakoff and Mark Johnson, *Metaphors We Live By* (Chicago: University of Chicago Press, 1980), 3-9.

90 Andrew Newberg and Mark Robert Waldman, *How God Changes Your Brain: Breakthrough Findings from a Leading Neuroscientist* (New York: Ballantine Books, 2009), 49-55.

91 Nicholas A. Christakis and James H. Fowler, *Connected: The Surprising Power of Our Social Networks and How They Shape Our Lives* (New York: Little, Brown and Company, 2009), 105-111.

92 Caroline Leaf, *Who Switched Off My Brain? Controlling Toxic Thoughts and Emotions* (Dallas: Switch on Your Brain, 2009), 55-62.

[93] Graham Cooke, *Developing Your Prophetic Gifting* (Grand Rapids: Chosen Books, 2003), 134-140.

[94] Gordon D. Fee, *God's Empowering Presence: The Holy Spirit in the Letters of Paul* (Peabody: Hendrickson, 1994), 827-833.

[95] Thomas Merton, *New Seeds of Contemplation* (New York: New Directions, 1972), 1-7.

[96] Darrell L. Bock, *Luke, Baker Exegetical Commentary on the New Testament* (Grand Rapids: Baker Academic, 1994), 1:478-484.

[97] Willem A. VanGemeren, ed., *New International Dictionary of Old Testament Theology and Exegesis* (Grand Rapids: Zondervan, 1997), 3:1185-1186.

[98] Walter Brueggemann, *The Message of the Psalms: A Theological Commentary* (Minneapolis: Augsburg, 1984), 73-79.

[99] Richard Rohr, *Everything Belongs: The Gift of Contemplative Prayer* (New York: Crossroad, 1999), 28-35.

[100] Michael Casey, *Sacred Reading: The Ancient Art of Lectio Divina* (Liguori: Triumph Books, 1996), 57-64.

[101] Henri J.M. Nouwen, *The Way of the Heart: Desert Spirituality and Contemporary Ministry* (New York: Seabury Press, 1981), 35-42.

[102] Alexander Schmemann, *For the Life of the World: Sacraments and Orthodoxy* (Crestwood: St. Vladimir's Seminary Press, 1973), 29-36.

[103] Cynthia Bourgeault, *Centering Prayer and Inner Awakening* (Cambridge: Cowley Publications, 2004), 5-12.

[104] Andrew Newberg and Eugene G. D'Aquili, *Why God Won't Go Away: Brain Science and the Biology of Belief* (New York: Ballantine Books, 2001), 113-120.

[105] Thomas Keating, *Open Mind, Open Heart: The Contemplative Dimension of the Gospel* (New York: Continuum, 1986), 11-18.

[106] Brother Lawrence, *The Practice of the Presence of God*, trans. *E.M. Blaiklock* (Nashville: Thomas Nelson, 1982), 27-34.

[107] A.W. Tozer, *The Knowledge of the Holy* (New York: HarperCollins, 1961), 1-7.

[108] Terence E. Fretheim, *Exodus, Interpretation* (Louisville: John Knox Press, 1991), 308-315.

[109] N.T. Wright, *The Challenge of Jesus: Rediscovering Who Jesus Was and Is* (Downers Grove: InterVarsity Press, 1999), 121-127.

[110] John Piper, *Seeing and Savoring Jesus Christ* (Wheaton: Crossway, 2004), 17-23.

[111] Michael Card, *A Sacred Sorrow: Reaching Out to God in the Lost Language of Lament* (Colorado Springs: NavPress, 2005), 127-133.

[112] Gregory of Nyssa, *The Life of Moses*, trans. *Abraham J. Malherbe and Everett Ferguson* (New York: Paulist Press, 1978), 94-101.

[113] Teresa of Avila, *Interior Castle*, trans. E. Allison Peers (New York: Doubleday, 1961), 87-94.

[114] Julian of Norwich, Showings, trans. Edmund Colledge and James Walsh (New York: Paulist Press, 1978), 175-182.

[115] Richard J. Foster, *Prayer: Finding the Heart's True Home* (San Francisco: HarperSanFrancisco, 1992), 155-162.

[116] Thomas à Kempis, *The Imitation of Christ*, trans. Leo Sherley-Price (London: Penguin, 1952), 83-90.

[117] Stanley Hauerwas, *The Peaceable Kingdom: A Primer in Christian Ethics* (Notre Dame: University of Notre Dame Press, 1983), 97-103.

[118] Miroslav Volf, *After Our Likeness: The Church as the Image of the Trinity* (Grand Rapids: Eerdmans, 1998), 213-220.

[119] Dietrich Bonhoeffer, *Life Together*, trans. John W. Doberstein (New York: Harper & Row, 1954), 26-33.

[120] Os Guinness, *The Call: Finding and Fulfilling the Central Purpose of Your Life* (Nashville: Word, 1998), 29-36.

[121] Gordon T. Smith, *Courage and Calling: Embracing Your God-Given Potential* (Downers Grove: InterVarsity Press, 1999), 23-30.

[122] Frederick Buechner, *Wishful Thinking: A Theological ABC* (New York: Harper & Row, 1973), 95-96.

[123] Henri J.M. Nouwen, *In the Name of Jesus: Reflections on Christian Leadership* (New York: Crossroad, 1989), 17-24.

[124] Parker J. Palmer, *Let Your Life Speak: Listening for the Voice of Vocation* (San Francisco: Jossey-Bass, 2000), 4-11.

[125] Eugene H. Peterson, *The Pastor: A Memoir* (New York: HarperOne, 2011), 126-132.

[126] Thomas Merton, *No Man Is an Island* (New York: Harcourt Brace, 1955), 112-119.

[127] Elisabeth Elliot, *Through Gates of Splendor* (Wheaton: Tyndale House, 1981), 236-243.

[128] Francis Brown, S.R. Driver, and Charles A. Briggs, *The Brown-Driver-Briggs Hebrew and English Lexicon* (Peabody: Hendrickson, 1996), 767-768.

[129] Walter Bauer, Frederick W. Danker, William F. Arndt, and F. Wilbur Gingrich, *A Greek-English Lexicon of the New Testament and Other Early Christian Literature*, 3rd ed. (Chicago: University of Chicago Press, 2000), 552-553.

[130] Peter T. O'Brien, *The Epistle to the Philippians, New International Greek Testament Commentary* (Grand Rapids: Eerdmans, 1991), 398-405.

[131] Peter H. Davids, *The First Epistle of Peter, New International Commentary on the New Testament* (Grand Rapids: Eerdmans, 1990), 56-62.

[132] Amy Carmichael, *Gold Cord: The Story of a Fellowship* (London: SPCK, 1932), 174-180.

[133] Henri J.M. Nouwen, *The Wounded Healer: Ministry in Contemporary Society* (New York: Doubleday, 1979), 82-88.

[134] John of the Cross, *Dark Night of the Soul*, trans. Mirabai Starr (New York: Riverhead Books, 2002), 59-65.

[135] Jeanne Guyon, *Experiencing the Depths of Jesus Christ* (Sargent: Christian Books, 1975), 132-138.

[136] Dietrich Bonhoeffer, *Letters and Papers from Prison*, ed. Eberhard Bethge (New York: Macmillan, 1971), 369-375.

[137] Corrie ten Boom with John and Elizabeth Sherrill, *The Hiding Place* (Washington Depot: Chosen Books, 1971), 215-221.

[138] Elisabeth Elliot, *A Path Through Suffering* (Ann Arbor: Servant Publications, 1990), 43-50.

[139] Jerry Bridges, *The Pursuit of Holiness* (Colorado Springs: NavPress, 1978), 18-25.

[140] Kenneth S. Wuest, *Wuest's Word Studies from the Greek New Testament* (Grand Rapids: Eerdmans, 1973), 1:178-179.

[141] J.I. Packer, *Keep in Step with the Spirit* (Grand Rapids: Revell, 1984), 95-102.

[142] John Ortberg, *The Life You've Always Wanted: Spiritual Disciplines for Ordinary People* (Grand Rapids: Zondervan, 2002), 43-50.

[143] Philip Yancey, *What's So Amazing About Grace?* (Grand Rapids: Zondervan, 1997), 181-188.

[144] Dallas Willard, *The Great Omission: Reclaiming Jesus's Essential Teachings on Discipleship* (New York: HarperOne, 2006), 61-68.

[145] Charles H. Spurgeon, *Lectures to My Students* (Grand Rapids: Zondervan, 1954), 339-346.

[146] C.S. Lewis, *Letters to Malcolm: Chiefly on Prayer* (New York: Harcourt Brace Jovanovich, 1964), 75-82.

[147] Anthony A. Hoekema, *Saved by Grace* (Grand Rapids: Eerdmans, 1989), 273-280.

148 G.K. Beale, *The Book of Revelation,* New International Greek Testament Commentary (Grand Rapids: Eerdmans, 1999), 1127-1134.

149 N.T. Wright, *Surprised by Hope: Rethinking Heaven, the Resurrection, and the Mission of the Church* (New York: HarperOne, 2008), 147-153.

150 Richard Baxter, *The Saints' Everlasting Rest* (London: Thomas Underhill and Francis Tyton, 1650), 23-30.

151 Thomas Aquinas, *Summa Theologica,* trans. Fathers of the English Dominican Province (New York: Benziger Brothers, 1947), I-II, q. 3, a. 8.

152 Jonathan Edwards, *"The End for Which God Created the World,"* in *The Works of Jonathan Edwards,* vol. 8, ed. Paul Ramsey (New Haven: Yale University Press, 1989), 526-532.

153 Teresa of Avila, *Christ Has No Body,* widely attributed, though possibly a modern adaptation of her writings rather than a direct quote.

154 C.S. Lewis, *Mere Christianity* (New York: Macmillan, 1952), 188-189.

155 Martin Luther, *Luther's Works,* ed. Jaroslav Pelikan (St. Louis: Concordia Publishing House, 1955), 25:260-265.

156 Richard J. Foster, *Celebration of Discipline: The Path to Spiritual Growth* (San Francisco: Harper & Row, 1978), 7.

157 John Clayton, *Sermons on Important Subjects,* vol. 3 (Philadelphia: Presbyterian Board of Publication, 1865), 237-244.

[158] James D.G. Dunn, *The Theology of Paul the Apostle* (Grand Rapids: Eerdmans, 1998), 398.

[159] The Didache 9.5, in *The Apostolic Fathers,* trans. Bart D. Ehrman, Loeb Classical Library (Cambridge: Harvard University Press, 2003), 431.

[160] Athanasius, On the Incarnation 54, in *Nicene and Post-Nicene Fathers,* Second Series, vol. 4, ed. Philip Schaff and Henry Wace (Buffalo: Christian Literature Publishing, 1892), 65.

[161] Martin Luther, *Commentary on Galatians,* trans. Erasmus Middleton (Grand Rapids: Kregel Publications, 1979), 133-140.

[162] John Calvin, *Institutes of the Christian Religion,* ed. John T. McNeill, trans. Ford Lewis Battles, Library of Christian Classics (Philadelphia: Westminster Press, 1960), 3.1.1.

[163] John Owen, *Communion with God,* ed. R.J.K. Law (Edinburgh: Banner of Truth, 1991), 9.

[164] Thomas Goodwin, *The Works of Thomas Goodwin,* vol. 4 (Edinburgh: James Nichol, 1862), 375-381.

[165] Richard Sibbes, *The Complete Works of Richard Sibbes,* ed. Alexander B. Grosart (Edinburgh: James Nichol, 1862), 2:177-183.

[166] Brother Lawrence, *The Practice of the Presence of God,* trans. E.M. Blaiklock (Nashville: Thomas Nelson, 1982), 27.

[167] Teresa of Avila, *Interior Castle,* trans. E. Allison Peers (New York: Doubleday, 1961), 206-213.

[168] John Wesley, *A Plain Account of Christian Perfection* (London: Epworth Press, 1952), 51-58.

[169] Phoebe Palmer, *The Way of Holiness,* with Notes by the Way (New York: Lane & Scott, 1850), 84-91.

[170] Marcus Peter Johnson, *One with Christ: An Evangelical Theology of Salvation* (Wheaton: Crossway, 2013), 45-52.

ABOUT THE AUTHOR

Randy Curtis Jr. brings nearly two decades of ministry experience to his role as Bible teacher and theologian. His scholarly focus on Second Temple Period literature, Supernatural Worldview of the Historical Hebrew and early Christian thought has shaped a distinctive approach to understanding Scripture, one that bridges ancient wisdom with contemporary spiritual formation.

Curtis's theological methodology combines rigorous academic study with practical application, seeking to equip believers not merely with knowledge but with a transformative understanding of their identity in Christ. His teaching ministry has consistently emphasized moving beyond surface-level religious practice toward deeper spiritual realities.

Drawing from years of study in ancient Hebrew and early Christian texts, Curtis has developed particular expertise in the theological concepts that shaped the New Testament church. This background informs his current exploration of union with Christ, a theme that runs throughout Scripture but has often been obscured by modern religious frameworks.

In Perfect Union, Curtis tackles what he considers one of the modern church's most profound yet neglected truths. Writing with the conviction of someone who has witnessed both the power and the neglect of this doctrine, he challenges readers to reconsider what it truly means to be "in Christ." His approach is both scholarly and accessible, inviting believers to discover the radical implications of their covenantal relationship with the Messiah.

Curtis's work emerges from a deep burden to see the church rediscover its supernatural identity and walk in the fullness of what God has provided through union with His Son. He lives with his wife and five children, where his theological insights are applied and refined in the daily realities of family life and pastoral ministry.

For booking:

Email:

randycurtis7@icloud.com

Follow the author on

Instagram:

@RTCJR_87

@RTCJR_87